D0969463

Be Your Own Sales Manager

Strategies and Tactics for Managing Your Accounts, Your Territory, and Yourself

ANTHONY ALESSANDRA
JIM CATHCART
JOHN MONOKY

A FIRESIDE BOOK
Published by Simon & Schuster
New York London Toronto Sydney Tokyo Singapore

FIRESIDE
Simon & Schuster Building
Rockefeller Center
1230 Avenue of the Americas
New York, New York 10020

Copyright © 1990 by Anthony J. Alessandra, Jim Cathcart,
and John Monoky

First Fireside Edition 1992

Designed by Irving Perkins Associates
Manufactured in the United States

5   7   9   10   8   6

Library of Congress Cataloging-in-Publication Data

Alessandra, Anthony J.
Be your own sales manager : strategies and tactics for
managing your accounts, your territory, and yourself /
Anthony Alessandra, Jim Cathcart, John Monoky.
p.   cm.
1. Selling.   2. Selling—Vocational guidance.
I. Cathcart, Jim.   II. Monoky, John.   III. Title.
HF5438.25.A39   1990
658.8'5—dc20   89-26660
CIP

Portions of this book are based on the 1984 Prentice Hall Press
book *The Business of Selling,* by Anthony Alessandra
and Jim Cathcart.

Dedicated to

our wives—Sue Alessandra, Paula Cathcart and
Andrea Monoky

and our children—Justin & Jessica Alessandra, Jim Cathcart, Jr.,
Sarah, David, Anne & John Monoky

Contents

Preface

The goal of this book is to show you how to build a clientele, not just make sales. We will focus on selling in a way that your customers will want to do business with you again and again.

To accomplish this, we are going against the current so you can see things from a totally different perspective. On your part, this will involve expanding your viewpoint and changing your vocabulary. You will need to see selling as what it really is ... a profession—one that rightfully belongs alongside the professions of law, medicine, consulting, and finance and requires more than just a gift of gab, a firm handshake, and a perpetual smile. The sales profession requires you to become proficient in all of the activities and skills listed under the sales bicycle on page 9.

Before you start feeling overwhelmed, let us assure you that it is not as hard as it sounds; however, it does require effort. Perhaps a salesperson should take an oath just as doctors and lawyers do. The oath would clarify the key requirements of the profession and serve as a constant reminder of the salesperson's responsibility. It would clearly state that this profession is not to be entered into casually or taken lightly because it is a career, not just a job.

The Salesperson's Oath

I choose to be a professional in the field of selling. I make this choice knowing that selling has many requirements.

Selling requires caring. In order to serve others and to help people own the right product or service to fill their needs, I must learn to identify their needs. I must be skilled in the twin arts of probing and listening, for one without the other is useless.

Selling requires planning and study. For my sales career to endure, it must be built on a foundation of solid planning for long-term and short-term success. I must study my products and services until I know them thoroughly. I must know exactly how each customer can benefit from the use of my products or services. I must study the selling skills that will allow me to help my customers own the right products for their needs.

Selling requires strength of character. There will be times when I am tempted to make an easy sale that does not benefit the customer. At these times I must have the strength of character to avoid the sale and act in my customer's best interest. I must be able, at all times, to say that I have advised the customer to do exactly what I would do if I were in his or her position.

Selling requires determination and persistence. Many on whom I call will not buy my products. I must believe unflinchingly in the law of cause and effect (every good act brings a reward, every bad act brings a consequence). If I make enough calls with a professional attitude on qualified customers, I will achieve my goals.

Selling is dependent on the free enterprise system and is an integral part of it. Selling is based on the premise that one person's knowledge, skills, and handiwork can benefit another. It is also based on the belief that those who provide a service should be compensated. Profit is the incentive that motivates improvement. Profit, whether financial or otherwise, is a part of ownership, and with ownership there is always responsibility.

Selling requires responsibility. I must recognize my responsibility to serve my client well, uphold the principles of this oath and my profession, improve my own knowledge and skills, and profit from my labors. When I earn their respect, it is my right, for I am a professional salesperson. In today's society, professionals are not measured by the business they are in but by the way they are in business.

Selling as a Long-Term Occupation

The American dream has always been to start at the bottom and make it to the top. We have been Horatio Algerized into thinking that climbing the corporate ladder is the road to fulfillment and success. Recent experience has shown that this is not necessarily so. One need not start at the bottom or make it to the top to be successful. Success in recent years has been redefined as the achievement of worthwhile goals and the realization of self-fulfillment while achieving them.

There is no "bottom" in the field of selling. A forty-year veteran and a one-week rookie are on the same level when they go in to see a customer. It is the level of professional skill that determines which one gets the sale.

Selling has no seniority system. Just because you have been around a long time does not mean you are more professional or successful than another. Some twenty-year sales veterans are said to have one year's experience repeated twenty times, while others grow with each passing month and reach higher levels of professionalism in a short time.

Is a Salesperson All You Will Ever Be?

In other occupations, a person who has mastered a certain job typically wants to move up to the next level. Thus, it is natural to be constantly building toward acquiring the boss' job—and then the next one above that.

Selling has no such process. It requires a different growth orientation. Rather than striving for the position of sales manager, you are striving to become a better salesperson. Being paid according to sales gives unlimited income potential to the professional who is dedicated to becoming a better salesperson.

This book is dedicated to making you a better and better salesperson. It provides all the information and techniques you need to run your selling career as a business—a highly successful, profitable, and ethical one.

Acknowledgments

In writing this book, we have drawn liberally from our previous articles, books, and hundreds of sales seminars throughout the world presented to thousands of salespeople selling countless tangible and intangible products and services.

We would like to thank the people who have contributed to the development and refinement of this book and those who have helped us grow as individuals. It is impractical to list all the mentors, teachers, role models, and friends who have touched our lives. We would, however, like to acknowledge a select few for their "special" contributions.

Vital input was received either directly or through the works of Steve Curtis, Merrill Douglas, Del Dowdell, Harold Gash, Fred Herman, Alan Lakein, Dr. John Lee, John T. Molloy, Earl Nightingale, Joel Weldon, Peter Wheeler, and Joe D. Willard.

Our completion of the manuscript depended heavily on the contributions of Marsha Field, Karen Morse, Terri Trotter, Debra Cook and Tom Hamway. Without their help you might be hearing this material on cassette rather than reading it.

Tony Alessandra, Ph.D.
Jim Cathcart, C.S.P., C.P.A.E.
John Monoky, Ph.D.

1

Salespeople Are Managers of Sales

THE premise of this book is that salespeople must assume many of the sales manager's responsibilities. Does this mean that sales managers are not doing their job? Perhaps. However, the fault may not be the sales manager's. Sellers promoted to sales managers may be ill prepared for the new job or not allowed to perform effectively in it.

Are Sales Managers Dinosaurs?

How much time has your sales manager spent coaching and counseling you in the field? How effective have your performance reviews been? How often has the information and directions provided by your sales manager been confusing or conflicting? How effective has your sales training program been in providing knowledge and skills that improve your performance? What criteria are you being measured on, and what constitutes performance? How efficient and equitable are the sales territories within your organization?

These questions may lead you to conclude that perhaps your sales manager is more of a superseller than a true sales manager. Jack Carew, in a recent issue of *Sales and Marketing Management* magazine, wrote "When Salespeople Evaluate Their Managers":*

"Ken, a sales representative, has just returned from a performance review with his manager, Jerry. Ken is still seething. It had gone something like this:

First his manager reminded him of the sales objectives that had been presented at the last regional meeting. Then Jerry blasted Ken for losing an account to a competitor. He insisted that Ken had to do more prospecting.

Jerry then announced that he would be taking over an account that Ken was developing because, as he explained it, "I foresee some problems, and I want to make sure we close on this one."

Finally, Jerry told Ken he was pleased with his progress. Despite some recent setbacks, he said, Ken was generally doing well. Now, if he would just get out there and open some new accounts. . . .

Ken's manager concluded with a warm, enthusiastic talk on how difficult it was to prospect, and how much disappointment was involved, but how sure he was that Ken would eventually be successful.

Sound farfetched? It's not. In fact, for thousands of sales professionals, scenes like this are all too common.

Although Ken must think he has the most insensitive, demanding, and erratic sales manager in the world, his situation is actually typical. And so is the dilemma of his manager—who probably finds himself with too many salespeople to manage, too large a district to administer, his own account responsibilities, steady pressure from above to increase sales, and a tide of paperwork and "administrivia" that threatens to overwhelm him at any moment. Given all this, it's no surprise—and

*Reprinted by permission of *Sales and Marketing Management*, copyright: March 1989.

no fault of his own—that Jerry's "management style" has become a hodgepodge of directives mixed with intimidation and persuasion, polished off with a brisk motivational talk."

Simply look at the way sales managers spend their time to get a sense of the burden and perhaps misdirection of your sales manager's efforts. A study initially conducted in the early 1970s by Rodney E. Evans has been updated several times by the authors. It basically addresses the issue "How do *sales managers* spend their time?":

Marketing Activities (19 percent)

- Analyzing sales data
- Communicating information to salespeople
- Digesting information from management
- Summarizing sales and customer data for management
- Reviewing competitive activity
- Forecasting future sales
- Reviewing sales coverage and salespeople territory alignment
- Advising on changes in price, delivery, arrangements, products, or new product development
- Managing advertising and/or other nonselling promotional activities
- Participating in the formulation of overall marketing policy

Selling Activities (36 percent)

- Making sales calls with salespeople
- Personal selling to own accounts
- Handling problem accounts
- Deciding on customer's request for special terms of sales
- Expediting customer orders
- Working with dissatisfied customers

Administration Activities (18 percent)
- Managing the field office
- Keeping records
- Writing reports on various aspects of district operations

Financial Activities (7 percent)
- Analyzing selling-expense data
- Controlling inventory and warehousing costs
- Controlling costs of branch office operation
- Watching the trend of costs expended in relation to profits generated
- Preparing budgets
- Advising on the need for additional capital expenditure

Personnel Activities (20 percent)
- Training salespeople
- Establishing standards of performance
- Planning and holding sales meetings
- Advising salespersons on personal problems
- Handling problem salespeople
- Recruiting and selecting new salespeople
- Revising people specifications for field sales
- Reviewing compensation programs for salespeople
- Forecasting future personnel needs

As you can see, 80 percent of the sales manager's time is spent doing work other than developing the sales team. The other activities are necessary and affect sales performance indirectly, except in the case of personal selling (36 percent).

This weakness in developing sellers is reflected in another study, this one conducted by *Industrial Distribution* with 10,000 industrial buyers. The conclusion was that today's salespeople have some serious deficiencies:

- 96 percent said the salespeople did not ask for a commitment for an order, apparently because they had lost control of the selling situation.
- 89 percent said the salesperson did not know his or her products.
- 88 percent said the salesperson did not present or demonstrate the products; what he or she appeared to be selling was price.
- 85 percent said that salespeople lacked empathy.
- 82 percent said they would not buy from the same salespeople or companies again and cited "neglect" and "indifference" as the major reasons.

A study of 257 Fortune 500 companies found that:

- 83 percent do not determine an approximate duration for each sales call.
- 77 percent do not use the computer to assist in time and territory management.
- 72 percent do not set profit objectives for accounts.
- 63 percent do not use prescribed routing patterns in covering territories.
- 54 percent do not conduct organized studies of their use of time.
- 51 percent do not determine the number of calls it is economical to make on an account.
- 51 percent do not use a prepared sales presentation.
- 30 percent do not use call schedules.
- 25 percent do not have a system for classifying customers according to potential.
- 24 percent do not set sales objectives for customer accounts.
- 19 percent do not use a call report system.

Before you condemn your sales manager or become overly sensitive about your own professionalism, recognize that you can take a greater degree of responsibility in the development of your own selling effectiveness. This book gives you the tools to overcome these shortcomings and put you on the path to the top of your profession. Rather than waiting and depending on your sales manager, it behooves you to take control of your own destiny.

Becoming Your Own Sales Manager

You can become a superstar simply by learning how to ride a bicycle. Not just any bicycle, mind you—the *sales* bicycle. And not just by riding it but by mastering the art of maneuvering it. You must learn how to move the pedals to get maximum drive from the back wheel and to move the handlebars to get accurate direction from the front wheel. When you can do that, you will reach the destination of success, in both earnings and prestige. Want to know more about the sales bicycle and how you can master riding it? Read on.

The back wheel of our sales bicycle represents the business skills that give your sales career drive. It consists of the self-management and sales planning skills that help you call on the right people at the right time with the right product or service. The back wheel skills (business side) of selling are the primary focus of this book.

The front wheel of the sales bicycle represents the interpersonal selling skills that provide you with direction. Sales communications and face-to-face selling techniques are front-wheel skills. More specifically, your sales communications expertise encompasses your verbal and nonverbal communications skills, as well as your ability to size up prospects and be flexible in communicating with them. Your face-to-face (relationship) selling skills include your expertise in telephone techniques and correspondence, creating favorable impressions (image), studying prospect needs and problems (information gathering), proposing relevant solutions (presentation), confirming the sale (commitment and implementation), and ensuring customer satisfaction (follow-through). They are covered in great detail in our other books, such as *Non-Manipulative Selling* and *Relationship Selling*.

The back wheel is the focus of *Be Your Own Sales Manager.* In order to utilize the front wheel's "Interpersonal Selling" skills effectively and efficiently, the back wheel's priorities, plans, and programs must be in place. Much of what falls into the back-wheel category has traditionally been the domain of the sales manager. You must take on the back-wheel responsibilities if you are to become a true professional.

Chapter 2 covers the values and goals of successful selling. Your personal plan for the future in terms of career, family, financial, mental, physical, social, and spiritual goals is the logical starting point in the process. Chapter 3 assesses the organization's goals and priorities as they affect you, the salesperson. What are your responsibilities? What are you being asked to do? To whom are you being asked to sell? What are the organization's product mix priorities?

Chapter 4 shows you how to begin to develop sales programs to achieve your personal goals, and the organization's goals and to develop satisfied clients/customers. Chapters 5 and 6 address the issues of positioning you to sell against competition by understanding the needs and behaviors of your customers and competitors.

Chapter 7, one of the cornerstones of this book, pulls together all of the previous material in the form of a territory plan. It provides explicit instructions on creating the sales plan through the development of an account portfolio, a territory plan, and an implementation schedule. The ideas and forms in this chapter alone could dramatically increase your sales effectiveness.

Chapter 8 develops your strategies and tactics for selling to your key accounts—those strategically important to both your short- and long-term successes.

Chapter 9 covers the crucial subject of prospecting. Without a good flow of qualified prospects, even the best face-to-face salesperson eventually fails. Sources of prospects and creative ways to reach them, qualify them, and monitor their progress from prospect to client are covered.

Chapter 10 provides you with the tools to measure and monitor your performance.

Chapter 11 addresses time management. Although the entire book will help you increase your productivity, which indirectly improves time management, this chapter provides tested methods that specifically address this issue.

Chapter 12 answers the question: "How do I keep myself motivated to do all this?" Carrying out the daily tasks that will eventually lead to your success as a seller is crucial. Sales are rewards in themselves in the form of remuneration. "Nice tries" and continuous effort are what motivation is all about. How can a sales manager motivate you if you can't motivate yourself?

The Appendix presents a useful methodology for estimating the opportunities in your territory. It will require an investment of time and energy on your part. As you work through this book, use your best estimate of your territory market potential. If you are uncomfortable with your guesstimate, we strongly urge the effort that this Appendix will require. It is well worth it!

When all this is set in motion, our sales bicycle will look like this:

Figure 1-1 *

BACK WHEEL DRIVE	FRONT WHEEL DIRECTION
"Managing to Sell"	**"Interpersonal Selling"**
SALES MANAGEMENT	SALES COMMUNICATIONS
Personal Goals	Verbal Communications
Organizational Goals	Nonverbal Communications
Marketplace Opportunities	How to "Size-up" People
SALES PLANNING/	(NON-MANIPULATIVE)
TARGET MARKETING	RELATIONSHIP SELLING
TERRITORY/TOTAL ACCOUNT	INDIVIDUAL ACCOUNT
MANAGEMENT	MANAGEMENT
Coaching	Meeting
Counselling	Studying
Training	Proposing
Evaluating	Confirming
Motivating	Assuring

Let's get on the sales bicycle and ride through the rest of this book together. We're sure you'll find this one of the most enjoyable and profitable trips you've ever taken.

---

* We would like to acknowledge Larry Wilson of the Wilson Learning Corporation as the person who popularized the bicycle/sales analogy.

Your Sales Career
and Your Life

FOR many years, people lived with the mistaken belief that their home life and their work could be totally separate. Many people gave their families and personal lives a back seat to their careers. For years they chased only the carrot of success while other facets of their lives suffered.

In the 1960s the pendulum began to swing in the other direction. Young people started questioning the traditional values of the establishment. They denounced the all-consuming work ethic and advocated recognizing people as individuals with needs that extend beyond work.

Balance

We all need to keep our lives in balance. Many needs must be fulfilled if we are to be well adjusted and happy. Our basic needs can be broken down into seven categories: mental, physical, family, social, spiritual, career, and financial.

In many ways we are like the fragile ecosystem in which we

live. The different elements of our lives are interdependent. One need affects the others, especially when it is grossly neglected. For example, financial problems affect personal outlook, health, social life, and family life. For this reason practitioners of holistic medicine examine all facets of a person's life when they search for the cause of a physical illness.

We are complex beings with complex needs. Our needs are dynamic rather than static—that is, they change. At one point in our lives, the development of a career may require more time than our spiritual or family needs. At some other time, physical needs may be emphasized more than social or financial needs. Just because one need is more urgent than others does not mean that the others disappear. All needs must receive at least a minimal amount of attention. Rarely can a need be completely neglected without unpleasant consequences.

To manage your sales career effectively, you need to work at bringing your life into balance. This requires *goal setting*— identifying the results you would like to achieve for each facet of your life. Only then can you plan the concrete goals and steps that stand between your current situation and your ideal concept of yourself.

If You Don't Know Where You're Going . . .

There's an old saying: "Most people aim at nothing in life . . . and hit it with amazing accuracy." It's a sad commentary about people, but it's true. It is the striving for and the attainment of goals that makes life meaningful. Lewis Carroll stated our point beautifully in *Alice in Wonderland*:

> ALICE: Mr. Cat, which of these paths shall I take?
> CHESHIRE CAT: Well, my dear, where do you want to go?
> ALICE: I don't suppose it really matters.
> CHESHIRE CAT: Then, my dear, any path will do!

No matter what kind of traveling you're doing—whether it's through your life or across the country by car—if you don't know where you're going, you'll never know if you've arrived. Taking just any road will leave your fulfillment to chance. That's not good enough.

People who have no goals feel emotionally, socially, spiritually, physically, and professionally unbalanced. This can only cause anxiety. People who have goals are respected by their peers; they are taken seriously. Making decisions that affect the direction of your life positively is a sign of strength. Goals create drive and affect your personality.

It is easy to spot a person who has a clear set of goals. That person exudes a sense of purpose and determination. He or she has abundant energy and is willing to put time and effort into any task. Being goal oriented helps you become more positive, optimistic, and assertive.

We can think of ourselves as bodies of water. Someone with no goals is like a stagnant lake—spread out, with no movement. The lake just sits motionless at the bottom of a mountain. A goal-oriented person is like a river forging its way through the mountains. The river has movement. It is exciting, and it carries things with it in its flow of enthusiasm.

In recent years many studies have focused on productivity. One repeatedly confirmed finding is that people who continuously set, pursue, and monitor their career goals are more productive than people who just work at a job. Pride in and ownership of one's choices are important ingredients in career satisfaction and success. The uninspired worker goes home at the end of the day, having gained nothing more than a few dollars and a lot of irritation.

Even on the factory-worker level, it has been shown that productivity will increase if a better incentive is provided for the worker. We all know that pieceworkers are more productive than salaried employees. This proves the WIIFM principle: What's in It for Me? The greater the rewards, the higher the drive to attain goals. The individual chooses the goals with the most desirable payoff.

Figure 2-1

SELLING FAILURES CAUSED BY PERSONAL NEEDS

Cause of Failure

Lack of initiative

Lack of enthusiasm

Salesperson too customer-oriented

Lack of personal goals

Lack of job satisfaction

Insufficient self-discipline

No interest in self-development

Lack of self-confidence

Personal problems

Dishonesty

Unfortunate appearance

Improper attitude

Lack of tact and courtesy

Gambling and drinking

C. A. Kirkpatrick and F. A. Russ, *Effective Selling,* Southwestern Publishing Co., Cincinnati, OH, 1981, p. 24.

Figure 2-1 illustrates some of the causes of failure in the selling profession that can be attributed to a lack of balance in personal needs.

The 3-Percent Solution

Time magazine reported on a national survey a few years ago that found that only 3 percent of those surveyed had written personal goals; 97 percent of the people had no goals at all or had only thought about them. They had not committed their goals to writing. Interestingly the 3 percent who had written goals were found to have accomplished much more than any of the 97 percent. Almost every speaker, writer, and educator in the area of sales agrees that committing goals to paper is a necessary step. Later in this chapter we'll have you write out a detailed description of your goals. If you take the time to do this, you'll stack the odds in your favor and be on your way to becoming one of the successful 3 percent.

The dividends reaped by investing in yourself are unlike any other found in the financial world. When you clarify your values and set goals in all the major areas of your life, the right roads appear in front of you like mirages in the desert— yet they are real. Choices become infinitely easier to make, and you've taken a giant step toward living a balanced life.

Self-Fulfilling Prophecies

When you stop operating under the assumption that things will go on as they are forever, you can then initiate some changes. More often than not, it is our assumptions that limit our options. Negative assumptions set up internal obstacles that automatically defeat us.

One of the most common negative assumptions in sales is, "I'll never get that account, so why should I waste my time?" If you assume you won't get an account, then you won't. Either you'll pass it by, or you'll predetermine the outcome by your attitude. Predetermining the outcome could be saying to the buyer, "You're not interested in this product, are you?" Ninety-nine times out of 100 she'll prove you right by saying "No."

The following negative assumptions in sales are not uncommon:

- "The economy is bad so people aren't buying."
- "I'll never make as much money as I want."
- "I'll never find a product or service I can honestly be enthusiastic about."
- "They don't need my product or service."
- "They won't like me."
- "I'm not smart enough."
- "They won't be able to afford my product or service."
- "I'll never call on X number of accounts per week."
- "A man will never buy from me." (for saleswomen)
- "A woman will never buy from me." (for salesmen)
- "People don't like salespersons."

This type of thinking usually becomes a self-fulfilling prophecy. You assume you can't do something, and then you act in ways that guarantee your failure. You've then reinforced your original assumption. This could go on and on until you quit sales altogether.

Positive Thinking

In recent years much criticism has been leveled at positive thinking, probably because it has been exploited and over-commercialized. The fact remains, however, that positive thinking works. If you're serious about succeeding in your chosen field, you must cultivate positive thinking as a habit.

Self-Confidence

Self-confidence is an indispensable part of achievement. It stems from the awareness of our intrinsic worth as individuals. We are blessed with an incredible amount of potential, most of it untapped. George Santayana once wrote, "Man is as full of potentiality as he is of impotence." Santayana's words imply that the choice is ours, which it is.

Self-confidence works best when it's based on self-respect rather than on comparisons of yourself with others. A wise friend once said to me, "Don't compare yourself to other people because you'll feel either pompous or bitter . . . and neither one is desirable." Our self-confidence has to exist in a vacuum, and it can. It feeds on the knowledge gained from discovering one's inner potential.

Stepping-stones to Greatness

Achievements come from awareness, which starts with evaluating your strengths and weaknesses in the light of your current situation. You then expand your assumptions to accept more goals for yourself. This leads you to expand your actions and eventually to achieve your goals. The model for this process is:

AWARENESS → BELIEFS → GOALS → PLANS → ACTIONS →
ACHIEVEMENTS

One step leads to another. After an achievement, you reevaluate yourself and find that each new feather in your cap makes you feel capable of accomplishing more and more. Your beliefs (assumptions) then expand, making more goals possible.

The effect gains momentum and grows like a snowball rolling downhill. In this way, greatness is achieved through small stepping-stones.

Self-Exploration

In order to explore yourself and have a better idea of your values, we've designed a personal inventory for you to fill out. It consists of seven pages, one for each facet of your life: mental, physical, family, social, spiritual, career, and financial. In each of these seven categories we'd like you to answer six questions. Your answers should be short phrases. (*Please note*: People have a tendency to read through a book without stopping to complete an exercise. If you want to derive the maximum value from this book you need to read *and* participate. So please stop at this time and do this exercise. You'll find it extremely valuable. And *remember*: This book is yours. Feel free to write in it or jot notes in the margins.)

Key Goal Action Plan
Mental

What is the goal I would like to achieve?

To increase memory retension

What are the potential obstacles that stand in my way?

method to achieve goal

Why do I want to achieve this? What's in it for me?

To better my personal + business life

What is my action plan? How will I specifically achieve this goal?

By using training tapes

What is my target date/deadline for achieving this goal?

Within 3 months from receiving tapes.

How and when will I measure my success?

By seeing how many customer Names I can remember

Key Goal Action Plan
Physical

What is the goal I would like to achieve?

I would like to Lose 100. Pounds

What are the potential obstacles that stand in my way?

Lack of willpower

Why do I want to achieve this? What's in it for me?

~~Try harder~~ So I Can Look Sexy + be health

What is my action plan? How will I specifically achieve this goal?

To follow the Susan Powter method

What is my target date/deadline for achieving this goal?

By Dec. 1995

How and when will I measure my success?

By scale + clothes size

Key Goal Action Plan
Family

What is the goal I would like to achieve?

To have 2 children

What are the potential obstacles that stand in my way?

Excess weight

Why do I want to achieve this? What's in it for me?

Children

What is my action plan? How will I specifically achieve this goal?

Lose weight

What is my target date/deadline for achieving this goal?

Feb 96

How and when will I measure my success?

when I have the first of any two children

Key Goal Action Plan
Social

What is the goal I would like to achieve?

To have more parties & make new couple friends

What are the potential obstacles that stand in my way?

Lack of resoures

Why do I want to achieve this? What's in it for me?

Popularity

What is my action plan? How will I specifically achieve this goal?

By going out to meet new People socialize

What is my target date/deadline for achieving this goal?

June 95

How and when will I measure my success?

By march 95

Key Goal Action Plan
Spiritual

What is the goal I would like to achieve?

To go to church & temple with Eric

What are the potential obstacles that stand in my way?

His Lack of Interest

Why do I want to achieve this? What's in it for me?

The future Spiritual Life of my children

What is my action plan? How will I specifically achieve this goal?

To attend Services alternating every other month

What is my target date/deadline for achieving this goal?

June 95

How and when will I measure my success?

Starting march 95

Key Goal Action Plan
Career

What is the goal I would like to achieve?

To succeed in my New Career

What are the potential obstacles that stand in my way?

Lack of Experience

Why do I want to achieve this? What's in it for me?

$

What is my action plan? How will I specifically achieve this goal?

By Learning as much as Possible

What is my target date/deadline for achieving this goal?

By Jan 95 —

How and when will I measure my success?

By paying off my debts & start a savings for my house

Key Goal Action Plan
Financial

What is the goal I would like to achieve?

To pay off all our Debts

What are the potential obstacles that stand in my way?

Lack of $

Why do I want to achieve this? What's in it for me?

No worries

What is my action plan? How will I specifically achieve this goal?

To have both Eric + I go to work

What is my target date/deadline for achieving this goal?

Dec 95

How and when will I measure my success?

when I am up to date on all my bills.

Figure 2-2

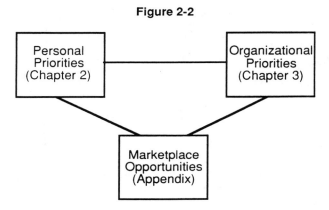

The values you've explored here compose one of the key-stone elements in the analysis of this book.

As you can see from Figure 2-2, Chapters 2 and 3 and the Appendix cover the analysis needed for professional development. The balancing of your personal priorities against your organization's priorities, in consideration of what can be accomplished in your marketplace, is the key to growth and success.

Career Priority

What do you want to accomplish in your professional career? Many types of selling professions can lead to other career paths such as management. And a career as a professional seller has many paths too. Figure 2-3 pictures the range of careers in selling . . . The choice is yours!

Figure 2-3

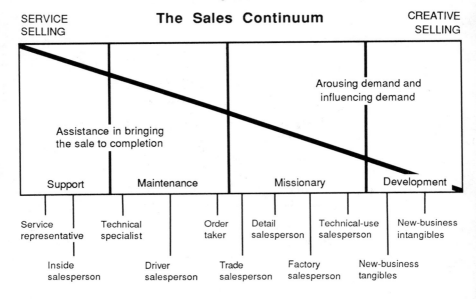

3

Organizational Goals and Priorities

THE next step in the process of becoming your own sales manager is to take stock of what your organization is asking of you. Even if you are selling for your own company, there is reason to evaluate the organizational priorities that must become part of your game plan. The personal goals and priorities that you evaluated in Chapter 2 must be consistent with your organization's direction.

The Job Description

The logical place to start the process of determining your organization's priorities for you is your job description . . . if you have one. If you don't, perhaps it would be a good idea to ask for one—or write your own.

The job description describes the tasks and duties associated with your position. It should also contain the criteria on which you will be judged.

One of the major reasons that salespeople fail to perform is a lack of clarity about their tasks. Are you really sure of what you are supposed to be doing? Are you overloaded with conflicting or ambiguous directions? You must realize that you are constantly being "told" what to do in your job by many different sources:

- Society in general
- Your company
- Your family
- Your customers
- Other members of the sales force
- Your sales manager
- Upper management

Unless you have your job clearly defined and understood, it can become difficult to succeed.

What exactly should go into your job description? A seller's job description contains the following qualitative elements:*

1. The *type of the products or services* to be sold.
2. The *types of customers* to be called on, including the policies concerning the frequency of calls on different types of customers, as well as the types of personnel within customer organizations who should be contacted (e.g., buyers, purchasing agents, plant supervisors).
3. The *specific tasks and responsibilities* to be carried out, including planning, research, and information collection activities; specific selling tasks; other promotional duties; customer servicing activities; and clerical and reporting duties.
4. The *relationships between the salesperson and other positions* within the organization. To whom does the job holder report? What are the salesperson's responsibilities to his

* Churchill, Ford, and Walker, *Sales Force Management, Third Edition*, Richard D. Irwin, Inc., Homewood, Illinois, Copyright 1990, page 417.

or her immediate superior? How and under what circumstances does the salesperson interact with members of other departments in the organization, such as production or engineering?

5. The *mental and physical demands* of the job, including the amount of technical knowledge the salesperson should have concerning the company's products, other necessary skills, and the amount of travel involved.

6. The *environmental pressures and constraints* that might influence performance of the job, such as market trends, the strengths and weaknesses of the competition, the company's reputation among customers, and resource and supply problems.

These six elements must be fully defined if you are to succeed.

You must also understand the quantitative results that you will be held accountable for producing. These are typically expressed as "output variables" such as:

- Gross sales
- Gross profit margin
- Share of market
- Product mix
- Sales budget
- Growth percentage
- Expenses
- New accounts

These output variables are what you are usually measured against, and they are usually a significant component of your compensation plan. It is extremely important that you have a thorough definition and understanding of how these criteria will be measured—and what constitutes success.

The combination of the qualitative inputs and the quantitative outputs basically defines the job you are being asked to perform. You have to understand both the input and output components. You can plan and manage the inputs, which in turn produce the outputs.

The questions you must initially ask of your organization, if you are to function as your own sales manager, are:

Mission Statement
What am I trying to get done? What is the role of personal sales in my company?

Identify Inputs and Outputs
What am I being asked to produce on the output side, and what inputs (tasks and activities) are critical to this production?

Performance Criteria
What criteria will be used to measure my performance?

Measurement of Criteria
How and when will I be measured on these criteria?

Standards of Performance
What are the goals and priorities of my organization in terms of my job?

The Planning Sequence

It is also important to understand the planning sequence in your organization. If you were to look at the various levels of planning in your firm in Figure 3-1 it might look something like this:

The question you must address is, "What are the implications of these various levels for me in the performance of my job?" Let's examine each of them.

Figure 3-1

```
┌─────────────────────────────┐
│       STRATEGIC PLAN        │
└─────────────────────────────┘
              │
              ▼
┌─────────────────────────────┐
│       MARKETING PLAN        │
└─────────────────────────────┘
              │
              ▼
┌─────────────────────────────┐
│         SALES PLAN          │
└─────────────────────────────┘
              │
              ▼
┌─────────────────────────────┐
│       TERRITORY PLAN        │
└─────────────────────────────┘
              │
              ▼
┌─────────────────────────────┐
│        ACCOUNT PLAN         │
└─────────────────────────────┘
              │
              ▼
┌─────────────────────────────┐
│          CALL PLAN          │
└─────────────────────────────┘
```

Strategic Plan

This plan sets the overall direction and tone of the organization. The very nature of the firm—its personality, so to speak—is addressed here. It is usually developed by top management on a three- to five-year planning horizon. The basic question addressed here is, "What is the company going to be when it grows up?"

Generally, salespeople are not privy to the details of this plan except in terms of a mission statement for the organization and perhaps some financial aspirations. This information is not critical for your performance in the short run.

Marketing Plan

The marketing plan is just one of several functional plans; however, it is by far the most important from the viewpoint of the salesperson. The marketing plan basically rolls out the strategic plan on a one- to three-year time frame. The basic questions addressed can be conceptualized in the product/market matrix in Figure 3-2.

This matrix is a useful tool and one that we will use in the remaining chapters. It is simple but extremely insightful. To begin, the two dimensions—product mix and market-target segment mix—define the seller's environment. The product mix is what each salesperson has to offer. The market-target

Figure 3-2

		THE MARKET-TARGET SEGMENT MIX			
		Market Target A	Market Target B	Market Target N	Horizontal Totals
T H E P R O D U C T M I X	Product Line 1				
	Product Line 2				
	Product Line N				
	Vertical Totals				Grand Total

segment mix is even more important in that it defines the audiences toward which you will direct your selling efforts. The marketing plan provides you with your offerings to the market and a definition of your market targets.

Within each of the relevant cells—for example, product line 1 in market-target A—another set of questions is addressed by the marketing plan. These concern:

- Distribution
- Pricing
- Promotion
- Competition

All of these areas are critical to you—the field seller. How will we bring our product to this market target? Directly or through an indirect channel using wholesalers, distributors, and dealers? Your job depends on the answer.

What is our pricing strategy in this segment? How will we promote our offering? Who is the competition, and what is its strategy?

You as a seller must know and understand the marketing plan in your firm. In most organizations, marketing managers develop this plan with inputs from the field via the sales manager, as well as other sources of information. You may have to involve yourself more in the market planning process if you are going to be your own sales manager. Your involvement at the corporate level may be difficult, but at the territory level it is an absolute must.

Sales Plan

The sales plan translates the marketing plan into a program for the sales force to implement. It is typically done by the sales managers and consists of structuring the sales team and developing sales forecasts and budgets. This plan directly affects you. Some of the basic strategic questions addressed include:

- The role of the salesperson
- The size of the sales force
- The organizational structure of the sales force
- The allocation of selling time (deployment)
- The way various segments and types of accounts will be handled (account management)

The sales plan should also address the following tactical issues:

- Recruiting and selecting salespeople
- Training salespeople
- Compensating salespeople
- Evaluating salespeople
- Motivating salespeople
- Coaching salespeople

We will come back to some of these issues in later chapters since you will be asked to assume some of these responsibilities.

Territory Plan

This is definitely your ball game. The process of utilizing information from the marketing plan and the sales plan in the development of a territory plan is key. "Plan your work and work your plan" takes on some real meaning if we can pull this information together. Chapter 8 goes into significant detail on this process and the next two planning levels.

Account Plan

Once again, one of the key planning components for you is your account plan. It must include significant detail for your key accounts. The remaining accounts in your territory port-folio also require strategies but in less detail.

Call Plan

The frequency of calls and their purpose are addressed in your call plan. This is the typical planning document that most sellers are familiar with. It is the last step in the sequence and one that has value only in conjunction with the previously mentioned plans.

Key Questions

You must address the following questions in order to under-stand your organization's expectations:

1. What is the mission of the sales force in my firm? What are we all about?
2. What components of the product mix am I being asked to sell, and what is the relative importance of each?
3. What market-target segments are we going after, and what is their relative priority?
4. How will my performance be measured? how fre-quently? on what criteria?
5. What constitutes good selling behavior, in terms of the input variables (tasks and activities)?
6. What is the marketing program for each market-target segment in terms of the product, distribution, promotion, and pricing strategies?
7. Are these organizational goals and priorities consis-tent with my personal goals and objectives?
8. Who am I competing against in each market-target segment?

4

Developing Your Territory Sales Program

THIS chapter focuses on the planning process at the macro level within your territory. Chapters 5 and 6 will go into more detail on the analysis of segments and competitors. Chapter 8 pulls it all together in a territory plan.

The Marketing Plan

The discussion in Chapter 3 regarding the levels of planning within your firm described the marketing plan. The same process that was used to develop the organizational marketing plan is appropriate for your territory.

The firm's marketing plan represents the overall strategy your company uses to identify and pursue promising markets. It includes the process of deciding the company's objectives, policies, resources, and strategies. An understanding of this process is invaluable to you for two reasons. First, it will show how your company attacks an entire market with the intention of penetrating it. Second, you will see what you must do in your sales territory. The principles of sales planning and territory management that you will apply are the same as those used by your company. Your plans, of course, will be on a smaller scale and will affect specific accounts in a particular area.

The Bird's-Eye View

For each product manufactured or distributed, a company must determine the following:

1. *Who* and *where* are the buyers? In other words, what are the *target markets*?
2. *How* do we get the buyers? What is the most effective way of letting the target know that the product exists?
3. *When* is the best time to present our product to the target market?
4. *How much* will the buyers pay? This must be looked at in absolute terms, as well as in comparison to competitors' pricing.
5. *Where* and *how* will the buyers purchase the product? Will credit be extended? Can the items be leased? How will the distribution be handled?
6. Is the customer satisfied after the purchase? Did the product satisfy his or her needs? What kind of service will be needed in the future?

A great deal of planning and research is needed to answer these crucial questions. Marketing specialists compile data to guide them in forecasting potential sales, setting goals and action steps, and recording the results. These plans are then passed on to other levels within the corporation for execution and evaluation. The market plan usually breaks down into four sections: situation analysis, objectives, strategy, and control. Let's look at how this market plan applies to the sales plan.

The Sales Planning Model

The sales plan is practically identical to the market plan except that it deals with one salesperson's territory rather than an entire market. If you think of your territory as a submarket, you will see that you must perform many of the same steps as your company does in its market plan. The sales plan has a two-stage planning process. The first stage concerns the territory in general. The second stage concerns the individual accounts and the strategies for selling them. Figure 4-1 depicts the stages of the sales plan.

The first stage assesses your selling opportunities and problems just as the marketing plan does. In your search for exploitable sales opportunities, study the following in step 1:

1. Your company and its products or services
2. The industry in general
3. The competition and their market penetration
4. The market potential in your territory
5. Business trends in different market segments

After this analysis you can set some realistic territory and sales objectives. These goals for step 2 would consider the following:

1. The most profitable products or services to sell
2. The accounts of weak competitors to pursue
3. Prime market segments in your entire territory
4. Groups of specific prospects to contact

Figure 4-1

TWO-STAGE SALES PLANNING PROCESS

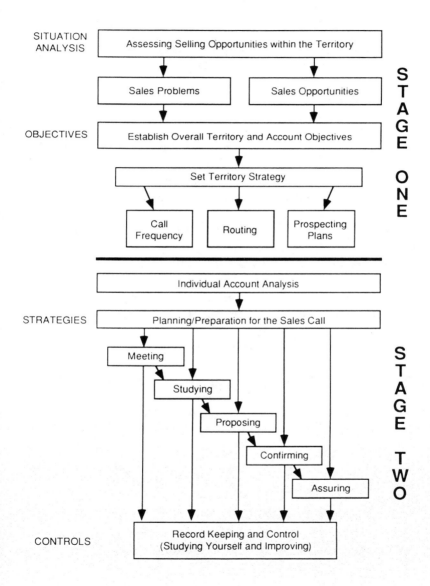

39

5. Objectives of total sales or volume for your entire territory and individual accounts

Step 3 is to develop strategies to accomplish the objectives you've set. These strategies will include:

1. Time management
2. Territory management

Territory management strategies include elements such as the frequency and priority of calls, methods of contacting prospects, promotional aids and prospecting plans. After all of this territory research has been completed, you can move on to the second stage.

Specific accounts are dealt with in step 4. Here the sales opportunities and strategies are analyzed account by account, giving special attention to the following:

1. Prospect's purchasing behavior and needs
2. Characteristics of the prospect's company
3. Overall industry the prospect is in
4. Actual or potential competition

This research will uncover a wealth of information, which can be used to great advantage when contacting a prospect or existing customer. Naturally sales and call objectives should be set for each account. These include both long-term and per-call goals. They can be as long range as "sell $100,000 worth of product X in the next year" or as short range as "introduce product at first meeting and schedule a demonstration."

Step 5 is the sales call itself:

1. Meeting with the prospect or client
2. Studying his or her needs
3. Proposing solutions

4. Confirming the sale
5. Ensuring effective solutions to his or her problems

Last, but not least, in the sales plan is step 6, the control phase. This is a nice way of saying that you'll be required to keep records of what you have done so that you can evaluate your performance later. Without the data provided by records, you will have no way of knowing if you accomplish your goals for the territory or individual accounts. Without this feedback, you will be unable to correct whatever problems you are having in achieving your objectives.

The two-stage planning process is a closed-loop system in which all stages depend on each other. All the information obtained in the control section is fed back to the situation analysis so that the process can begin again. This is a cycle that successful salespeople go through on a yearly or semiannual basis. The time taken to plan the strategies carefully for a given period of time will pay off in increased sales and increased awareness of what is being done correctly or incorrectly. This will turn the art of selling into a science for you.

Situation Analysis

Today's business climate is in constant flux, changing from week to week with the whims of a capricious economy or competitor. These rapid changes necessitate periodic assessments of the sales territory. By systematically and exhaustively assessing your sales problems and opportunities, you will have the knowledge necessary to maximize your time and efficiency.

Company Knowledge

Your company is the entity that stands behind the product or service you are selling. Initially customers may be more interested in your company than in you or the product. You must be knowledgeable enough to educate your client if you want to gain his or her trust and confidence.

Company knowledge is independent of product knowledge. You need to be familiar with the history and development of both. If you are a sales rep carrying many products, becoming familiar with each company may seem like an arduous task. You should, however, do it conscientiously.

Often a company describes its history, development, and philosophy when you begin working for it. If it does not, you can approach marketing or sales managers and ask for the information. If there are gaps in the information your company has given you, seek out the knowledgeable people and tell them your needs. Often engineers, executives, and others in high-level positions know more than those who sell the products. You should also be aware of your company's operating activities. Is it buying new subsidiaries or creating new divisions? How well is its stock doing on the market? Have there been any significant managerial or executive changes lately? If so, how will this affect the company's policies? All of this information is worth knowing so you will not be embarrassed if a customer asks you a question you cannot answer. Your knowledge will indicate to your client that you care about your firm and that you do business in an enlightened and professional manner.

Product Knowledge

Every company provides its salespeople with information about the product they will sell: brochures, specification sheets, and other printed materials. In addition, many companies offer training sessions, workshops, and other informative classes to bring their staff up to date on the latest developments in their products. All of this information is extremely valuable and should be absorbed voraciously by the salesperson.

As technology develops at phenomenal rates, product cycles become shorter and shorter. What is new today is obsolete tomorrow. More often than not, salespeople know more than their customers about these changes. They must introduce product changes to customers in a way that is informative as well as attractive. The growing need for salespeople to keep abreast of industrial changes is illustrated by the fact that salespeople in the digital watch, calculator, and video game industries spend as much as 50 percent of their time just learning about their products.

Some sales representatives carry more than one product. For them, the task of organizing products and becoming knowledgeable about each is made more difficult. A salesperson who carries three lines must do three times as much work to know all those products.

Look at the questions in Worksheet 4-1. Answer all of the questions in as much detail as possible. Many of these areas will be addressed in detail in later chapters.

Worksheet 4-1.
Company/Product Knowledge: Critical Questions
Part 1: *Company*

1. List the key personnel of your company and their unique contributions to the firm.

2. What unique capabilities or technical advantages does the company have?

3. What is the company's image and reputation among:
   • Current customers?
   • Prospects?
   • The competition?

4. What are its relative strengths and weaknesses compared to the competition?
   How do these affect business?

5. What is the marketing philosophy of your company?

6. What are the present and future markets of your company?

7. What has the company's sales history been during the last three to five years?

8. What is your company's standard policy regarding:
   - Pricing?
   - Discounts?
   - Guarantees?
   - Service?
   - Negotiating?

Part 2: *Product*

1. What specific benefits do current and prospective customers seek in your product?

2. How does your product compare to the competition's in providing those benefits?

3. Are there any features that make your product better than the competition's? If so, why?

4. How does your product compare to the others in your territory in the following aspects:
   - Quality?
   - Price?
   - Delivery?
   - Value added?
   - Reliability?

15. What factor(s) might prevent a customer from purchasing your product? What can you do about it?

6. Is your company a leader (developer) or follower (imitator) in its field?

Territory Knowledge

A major portion of your situation analysis has to do with your territory profile. Once again, the best way we have found to develop territory information is by the use of our old friend, the product/market matrix. Each cell in the matrix should be analyzed in the context of the following factors:

- Economic trends
- Technological trends
- Political/legal trends
- Competitive trends
- Industry trends

These factors will provide an evaluation of the problems and opportunities in your territory.

Economic Trends
Economic fluctuations and business cycles affect every business. Although the turning points in economic cycles are irregular, it is possible to anticipate them. Your estimate of the timing and magnitude of economic fluctuation will help prepare for probable variations in your business activity.

Your analysis of the economic climate should consider three levels: (1) local, (2) regional, and (3) national. The following specific indicators are useful in completing your analysis of the economic environment:

Element	Impact
Interest rates	Corporate spending, housing, construction, consumer durables
Unemployment	Consumer spending—nonnecessities, durable goods
Industrial production	Corporate spending, changes in unemployment

Element (*cont.*)	Impact (*cont.*)
Corporate profits	Corporate spending, employment levels, and, hence, an indirect impact on consumer spending
Inflation	All areas of spending
Consumer income	Consumer spending, especially non-necessities

This analysis should consider the direct impact on your business, as well as the indirect impact based on the effect of the economic climate on your customers.

Sources of information include your local chamber of commerce, newspapers, business publications, trade journals, and your trade association. Worksheet 4-2 contains a useful summary of these elements and your estimate of their impact on your territory. Add any categories that may be unique to your industry or type of business.

Technological Trends
Technology has been the most rapidly changing element in the business environment over the past decade. Technology increases your operating productivity. Also, the emergence of new products resulting from new technology translates into expanded product offerings.

In analyzing the role of technology in your business environment, consider the types of technology originating within your industry, as well as those outside your immediate industry. An analysis of technology should consider its impact on product lines carried and how it will improve operating efficiency.

List technical changes taking place both within and outside your industry. Primary information sources include business journals, trade publications, university/college sources, suppliers, and customers. Identify the effects, if any, they will

Worksheet 4-2

ANALYSIS OF ECONOMIC FACTORS

Evaluate in general terms the economic trends and their probable direct and indirect impact on your business.

Factor		Trend	Implication for Our Business	Impact on Key Market Groups	Threat/ Opportunity
1. General Economy	Local				
	Reg.				
	Natl.				
2. Unemploy-ment	Local				
	Reg.				
	Natl.				
3. Production	Local				
	Reg.				
	Natl.				
4. Corporate Profits	Local				
	Reg.				
	Natl.				
5. Inflation	Local				
	Reg.				
	Natl.				
6. Consumer Spending	Local				
	Reg.				
	Natl.				
7. Interest Rates	Local				
	Reg.				
	Natl.				

KEY: + Increasing   – Decreasing   0 Holding steady

have on product lines and internal operations and the overall implication for your business. Worksheet 4-3 summarizes your analysis of technological trends.

Political/Legal Trends

Government plays an ever-increasing role in determining how firms approach the market. A familiarity with proposed government action will enable you to adapt programs under *your* direction rather than under government edict.

What the government does is not necessarily a threat to your operations. In many instances, government action is a source of opportunities. By monitoring this segment of the environment, you will be able to gain advance notice of pending legislation and thus prepare accordingly.

Analyze the political/legal environment at three levels: (1) federal, (2) state, and (3) local. The primary sources of information include your state congressperson, trade publications, suppliers, key customer groups, regional newsletters, and your trade association. Worksheet 4-4 is provided for this purpose.

Competitive Trends

It is critical to realize that no business is an island or has a timeless, unrestricted claim on any market. In today's dynamic marketplace, competitive forces are always at work vying for a portion of your market or actively cultivating potential growth markets. One of the major thrusts of your situation analysis should be a detailed evaluation of primary competitors. This analysis should focus on the development of competitive profiles that clearly spell out each competitor's respective strengths and weaknesses. Chapter 6 will go into greater detail in this analysis.

Because of legal restrictions and competitive relationships, it will usually be impossible to interview your competitors' personnel directly. There are, however, other means of ob-

Worksheet 4-3

ANALYSIS OF TECHNOLOGICAL FACTORS

Origin	Technological Changes	Effect	Implications for Our Business	Implications For Customers	Threat/ Opportunity
1. Within Industry					
A. Products Carried					
B. Internal Operations					
1. Outside Industry					
A. Products Carried					
B. Internal Operations					

Worksheet 4-4

ANALYSIS OF POLITICAL FACTORS

Level	Proposed Legislation	Effect	Implications for Our Business	Implications For Customers	Threat/ Opportunity
1. Federal					
2. State					
3. Local					

53

taining information regarding competitors. Competitor profiles may be based on interviews of your own salespeople, suppliers, key customers, lending institutions, and others. Sources such as news clippings, journal articles, and advertising may provide valuable information. The following table provides a further listing of information sources from which to construct your competitor profiles:

	Public	Trade Professionals	Government	Investors
What competitors say about themselves	Advertising Promotional materials Press releases Speeches Books Articles Personal changes Want ads	Manuals Technical papers Licenses Patents Courses Seminars	Reports of the Securities and Exchange Commission Testimony Lawsuits	Annual meeting Annual reports Prospectuses Stock/bond issues
What others say about them	Books Articles Case studies Consultants Newspaper reporters Environmental groups Consumer groups Unions Who's Who Recruiting firms	Suppliers/ vendors Trade press Industry study Customers Subcontractors	Lawsuits State/ federal agencies National plans Government programs	Security analyst reports Industry studies Credit reports

Identify your major competitors within each market segment. Know key personnel, the number of employees, an estimate of sales, primary and secondary product lines, customer focus, and a detailed evaluation of their approach to the market (Worksheets 4-5 and 4-6).

Worksheet 4-5

ANALYSIS OF COMPETITORS

Product _____

Competitor	TARGET MARKET SEGMENTS				
1.					
2.					
3.					
4.					
5.					
6.					
7.					
8.					
9.					
10.					

Worksheet 4-6

ANALYSIS OF COMPETITORS

COMPETITOR PROFILE.   Complete this worksheet for each competitor
operating in your market/product segments.

Company _____

Location _____

Markets Served _____

KEY PERSONNEL

Name _____   Title _____

Name _____   Title _____

Name _____   Title _____

Number of Employees _____   Estimated Sales _____

Inside Sales Personnel _____   Outside Sales Personnel _____

Size of Facility _____ sq. ft.

Product Lines _____   _____

_____   _____

_____   _____

_____   _____

Marketing Approach

_____

_____

_____

_____

Appraise competitors' strengths and weaknesses within each market segment and product specialty area you serve. Also prepare a summary evaluation of your strengths and weaknesses within these segments relative to your competitors (Worksheet 4-7).

Industry Trends

Many industry conditions and trends will have an impact on market position, growth, and profitability. Your analysis should be conducted at two levels: (1) local and (2) national.

Review what is known about your industry in terms of trends that will have an impact on each market segment. Briefly describe the trend and evaluate the likelihood that the trend or condition will occur or continue (Worksheet 4-8).

Summary of Environmental Trends

You have developed a substantial fact base regarding trends in the external environment that affect your territory. The purpose of this section is to provide a capsulized picture of the marketplace in terms of key threats and opportunities that may have an impact on your business. In formulating strategies to combat potential threats and take advantage of emerging opportunities, consider not only the source of the threat or opportunity but also the timing of such events.

Review Worksheets 4-2 through 4-8. As you do, identify the sources of threats and opportunities and their likelihood of occurrence during the following time periods:

1. Long term (five to ten years)
2. Intermediate term (two to four years)
3. Short term (within one year)

Use Worksheet 4-9 for this purpose.

Worksheet 4-7

ANALYSIS OF COMPETITORS

STRENGTH/WEAKNESS PROFILE.   Complete this worksheet for each competitor operating in your market/product segments.

Market Segment _____

Company Name _____

CATEGORY	STRENGTHS	WEAKNESSES
Personnel		
Marketing Approach		
Pricing Policies		
Promotional Efforts		
Customer Image		
Customer Service		
Financial Strength		
Products		

Worksheet 4-8

ANALYSIS OF INDUSTRY TRENDS

Description of Trend or Condition	Likelihood of Occurrence	Market Segment(s) Affected	Impact On Sales
1.			
2.			
3.			
4.			
5.			
6.			
7.			
8.			
9.			
10.			

Worksheet 4-9

SUMMARY OF EXTERNAL THREATS AND OPPORTUNITIES

Time Period	Source	Opportunities	Threats
Long Term 5–10 years			
Intermediate Term 2–4 years			
Short Term Within 1 year			

Analyzing Last Year's Results

The situation analysis you conducted gave you a statement of your current problems and opportunities. Now you have to look at your prior year's results and your sales objectives in order to formulate your selling strategy.

Once again, use the product/market segment matrix for your analysis. For each cell develop the following:

1. Actual sales this year
2. Estimated market potential this year
3. Estimated market share this year
4. Source of sales this year (type of customer)
5. Estimated market potential next year
6. Tentative market share next year
7. Tentative sales objective (market-product combination)
8. Allocation of selling time by product and type of customer

Worksheet 4-10 combines several of the prior years' results and next year's data into a segment overview.

Worksheet 4-11 evaluates the source of your current year's sales by category of account: existing customers and new customers.

Worksheet 4-12 projects the source of your coming year's sales by category of account: existing customers and new customers.

The key is to translate these output measures (sales, market share) into inputs. The most logical way to do this, in our experience, is to translate these objectives into the item that you can control: your time.

After evaluating the changes in your current year's production (and perhaps even some prior years as well) and the

Worksheet 4-10

CURRENT AND COMING YEAR PERFORMANCE

Market Segment _____

	CURRENT YEAR		COMING YEAR			
Product Line	Estimated Market Potential Current Year	Actual Sales Current Year	Estimated Market Potential Coming Year	Sales Objectives Coming Year	Market-Share Objectives Coming Year	Change In Market Share Coming Year
1.						
2.						
3.						
Totals						

Worksheet 4-11

SOURCE OF CURRENT YEAR'S SALES 19____

MARKET SEGMENT _____

Product Line	Existing Customers	New Customers	Total
1.	_____ $ _____ %	_____ $ _____ %	_____ $ __100__ %
2.	_____ $ _____ %	_____ $ _____ %	_____ $ __100__ %
3.	_____ $ _____ %	_____ $ _____ %	_____ $ __100__ %
Total	_____ $ _____ %	_____ $ _____ %	_____ $ __100__ %

Worksheet 4-12

SOURCE OF COMING YEAR'S SALES 19____

MARKET SEGMENT _____

Product Line	Existing Customers	New Customers	Total
1.	_____ $ _____ %	_____ $ _____ %	_____ $ _100_ %
2.	_____ $ _____ %	_____ $ _____ %	_____ $ _100_ %
3.	_____ $ _____ %	_____ $ _____ %	_____ $ _100_ %
Total	_____ $ _____ %	_____ $ _____ %	_____ $ _100_ %

64

Worksheet 4-13

ALLOCATION OF SELLING TIME

Market Segment _____

Product Line	A.		B.		C.		TOTAL
	Existing Customers	Prospective Customers	Existing Customers	Prospective Customers	Existing Customers	Prospective Customers	
A. ___	___ %	___ %	___ %	___ %	___ %	___ %	___ %
B. ___	___ %	___ %	___ %	___ %	___ %	___ %	___ %
C. ___	___ %	___ %	___ %	___ %	___ %	___ %	___ %
D. ___	___ %	___ %	___ %	___ %	___ %	___ %	___ %
TOTAL	___ %	___ %	___ %	___ %	___ %	___ %	100 % ←

YOUR TOTAL SELLING TIME

projection for next year's results, determine how and where you will spend your selling time. How will you allocate your time to segments, products, and types of customers? These priorities will provide the base for developing your territory action plan. It will affect your call frequencies to existing accounts, as well as the amount of time spent prospecting.

Worksheet 4-13 allocates your selling time to these various categories. Your total selling time is represented by 100 percent. Allocate your time based on the percentage you feel is necessary in order to achieve your forecasted results. Once you have determined the total number of calls and/or selling hours you will have available next year, you can use the percentages to set up benchmarks of actual units of time for each category.

5

Understanding the Target Market Segments

Your organization has defined and targeted market segments in its marketing plan. Your job is to bring those programs and strategies to the street. In your territory, the segments may be more or less attractive than they might have been at the national or regional level. You need to develop a segment portfolio based on your perception of each segment's importance and you and your firm's ability to create a competitive differential in it.

The next step is to develop an understanding of the buying behavior in those targeted segments. You should address such elements as:

- Features and benefits
- Type of purchase
- Sales cycle
- Buying participants
- Decision-making criteria
- Decision-making process
- Decision-making roles

This same logic will be applied on an account-by-account basis in Chapter 9. At this stage we are using it to understand the market segments better.

Segment Portfolio

The logic of the segment portfolio is found in the Boston Consulting Group's (BCG) growth-share matrix. It is primarily used as a strategic planning tool at the corporate level, but it is appropriate with some modification at the territory level.

The BCG model has the market growth rate on the vertical axis and the relative market share on the horizontal. *Market growth rate* refers to the annual rate of growth of the market in which the business unit's products are sold. *Relative market share* refers to the business unit's market share relative to that of the largest competitors. The matrix that results from these two dimensions is presented in Figure 5-1. The terminology used to describe each of the cells is widely used and may be familiar to you.

Briefly, a *Star* is a high-growth/high-share business unit. It requires significant investments of time, energy, and promotional dollars. This is the future of your firm if it continues to grow and remain profitable. *Cash Cows* are low-growth/high-share business units. Stars become Cash Cows when growth slows. Cash Cows produce a lot of money to fund other programs and pay bills. *Question Marks* are low-share/high-growth situations. They require a decision on the part of management either to grow them by investing time, money, and effort or to divest them from the portfolio. If you fail to increase market share, they will become Dogs when the market growth slows. *Dogs* are low-growth/low-share business units. They are no longer growing, and you don't have any strength of position. The focus on this cell is to maintain self-sustaining profitability.

We will use this model in this chapter on market segments

Figure 5-1

and in Chapter 8 on accounts, but with a slight modification. Instead of rate of growth on the vertical, we will use *Segment Attractiveness*. On the horizontal, we will use *Strength of Position* instead of market share.

Segment Attractiveness takes into account any variable that would make that market segment of interest to your sales efforts. You should use factors such as these:

- Growth rate
- Size (potential)
- Degree of competition
- Profitability
- Potential market share
- Financial ability
- Need for your products/services
- Strategic importance of segment

The Strength of Position is a composite of several factors; all relate to your firm's ability to develop and maintain selling relationships with these segments. Typical measures used in this evaluation are:

- Current product concentration
- Share of market
- Experience in segment
- Knowledge of segment
- Relationships
- Contacts

In both measures, feel free to add or delete any variables that do not fit your situation and circumstances.

Worksheet 5-1 allows you to identify and quantify your perception of each segment's attractiveness. List the variables you feel are appropriate for this measurement in your territory in the column labeled "Segment Attractiveness." List by name the segments you could possibly sell your products to across the top. Then rate each market segment on each variable using this scale:

1 = Very negative
2 = Negative
3 = Neutral/Don't know
4 = Positive
5 = Very positive

Worksheet 5-2 is similar except you are assessing your selling strength. Use variables that are appropriate for measuring this component. Rate yourself in each of the segments that you have listed.

On both worksheets, add up the ratings that you have given to each segment. This will give you two scores for each segment: a score for Segment Attractiveness and a score for Strength of Position.

Worksheet 5-1

EVALUATING MARKET SEGMENT ATTRACTIVENESS

Market Segments

Segment Attractiveness						
Total Score						

Ratings: 1 Very negative
2 Negative
3 Neutral / Don't Know
4 Positive
5 Very Positive

Worksheet 5-2

EVALUATING STRENGTH OF POSITION

Market Segments

Segment Attractiveness						
Total Score						

Ratings: 1 Very negative
2 Negative
3 Neutral / Don't Know
4 Positive
5 Very Positive

These two scores should then be plotted on Figure 5-2. The position in one of the four cells will give you a good picture of your segment portfolio.

Those segments that fall in cell 1 are your Stars. They are your core segments in terms of their attractiveness, as well as your capabilities to be a major player. Cell 2 is segments that might become Stars if you selectively pick and then build enough critical mass to improve your strength of position. The segments in cell 3 constitute your Cash Cows. They are no longer as attractive as they once were, but based upon your strength with them, they can be an excellent source of sales and profits. The key is not to overspend on them. Cell 4 contains your candidates for divestiture from your segment portfolio. These Dog segments will have used your time and money with no appreciable return on the investment.

Now that you have sorted out your territory at the segment level, it makes sense to start to improve your knowledge and selling strategies for each segment.

Portfolio Characteristics

Each of the four cells in your portfolio has some unique characteristics.

Stars

You should have quite a few active accounts in your Star segments. Your account coverage should focus on your existing customers with an eye to increasing the number of new accounts in these segments.

Your approach will focus on problem solving and consultative selling. Service will also be of significant importance, and you will have to develop many marketing support programs for these accounts. Give this segment a significant amount of your time.

Figure 5-2

SEGMENT PORTFOLIO

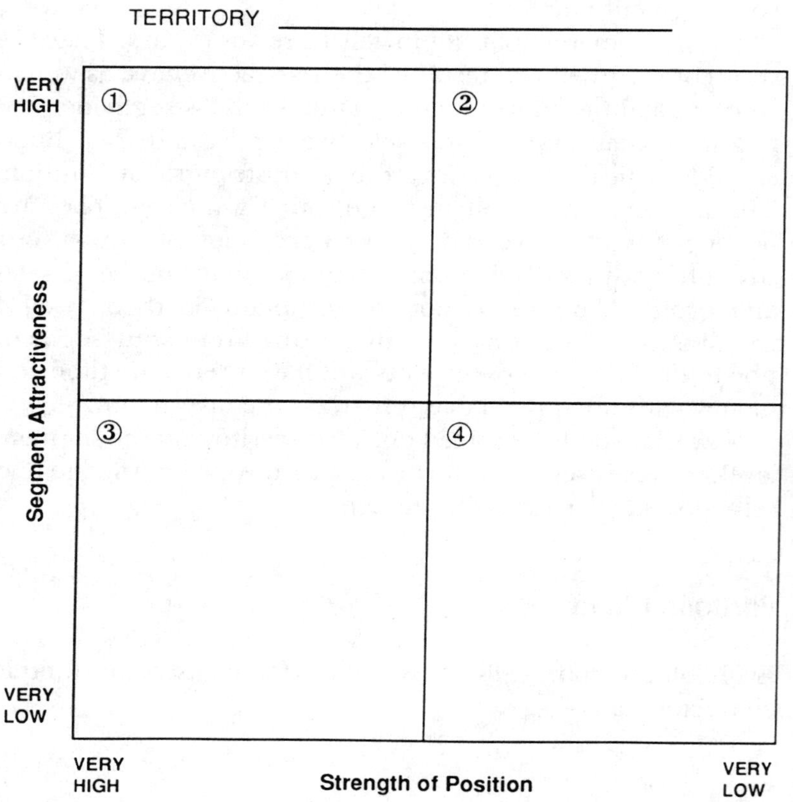

TERRITORY _____

VERY
HIGH

①   ②

③   ④

VERY
LOW

Segment Attractiveness

VERY
HIGH   **Strength of Position**   VERY
LOW

Question Marks

There should be fewer accounts in this category. Your key here is to identify new accounts in these segments selectively and improve your selling position so that they can be converted. The accounts in this category are probably your competitor's key accounts. Your primary strategy should be to identify needs that are not being fulfilled. Marketing programs and service levels should be carefully provided to these targeted accounts. This category should be allocated a small percentage of your selling time and a good portion of your research efforts.

Cash Cows

These segments constitute a large percentage of your current customer base. They were your Stars at one point and have become less attractive over time. Don't overinvest in time, programs, and service. While you should not ignore these accounts, you must maintain regularity only to the extent that they are willing to pay in terms of sales and profit margin dollars. Some of the contact time should be delegated to other parts of your sales team, such as inside salespeople if available. The telephone becomes an important tool for these accounts. Constantly reevaluate Cash Cow accounts and drop those that are not paying their way. This category should free some selling time that you can redirect toward your Stars and selected Question Marks.

Portfolio Knowledge

The portfolio concept also allows you to direct your research efforts toward the segments that are your future: the Stars and the targeted Question Marks. What should you know about these categories of accounts? You already have screened the external environment in Chapter 4. You must now start to address more specific questions:

1. What do they buy?
2. When do they buy?
3. How do they buy?
4. Who does the buying?
5. Who else can they buy from?
6. How do they obtain information?

What Do They Buy?

This seems to be an obvious question with an obvious answer: they buy what you sell, or you would not be spending so much time on them. However, in today's competitive marketplace, you have to know and understand more than the features of your products. The old saying about "manufacturing features and selling benefits" is true. That is what your clients purchase—benefits. What do they mean by "benefits"? Do all segments and customers within those segments have the same definition of benefits?

One way to address this question is to separate the "product" into three concentric circles:

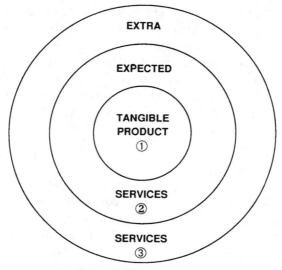

B. Merrifield, *Understanding the Dynamics of Industrial Distribution* (MCG,Inc., 203-661-1760).

Circle 1 represents the tangible product that you sell—the features. They can be touched, smelled, and seen. This is basically what all of your direct competitors sell. Specifications detailing the height, weight, density, tolerance, and other attributes can be obtained from your customers if they are familiar with their problems and solutions. If they do not fully understand or even know they have a problem, then you become the consultative seller to influence these tangible product specifications.

The second circle includes basic expected services—delivery, installation, warranty, engineering, and so forth. Since services have no measure of quality except in the eyes of the beholder, you can differentiate your offering at this expected service level. By understanding the nature and degree of these services and then striving for service excellence, you can create a strong relationship with your customers.

The outermost circle—extra services—contains those intangibles that are not for all of your customers. They may not even be expected until you raise your customer's level of understanding. These services go beyond the basics. Your job is to understand how your customers perform the total task of what they are trying to accomplish through the use of your "product." According to T. Levitt: "The new competition is not between what companies produce in their factories, but between what they add to their factory output in the form of packaging, services, advertising, customer advice, financing, delivery arrangements, warehousing, and other things that people value."*

Use worksheet 5-3 to identify and determine the importance of the various selection criteria that your target segments use to evaluate competitive offerings. We have provided twelve examples of the criteria that might be used. Add or delete categories as you see fit. Once you have developed your list, rate all of your target segments according to their perceptions of the relative importance of each criterion.

* T. Levitt, *The Marketing Mode* (New York: McGraw-Hill, 1969).

Worksheet 5-3

ANALYSIS OF KEY MARKET SEGMENTS

IMPORTANCE RATINGS: Evaluate the importance of each of the following selection criteria. Complete this worksheet for each segment.

MARKET SEGMENT: _____

	IMPORTANCE		
Selection Criteria	1 Not Important	2 Important	3 Very Important
1. General reputation			
2. Quality of products carried			
3. Range of products carried			
4. Prices of product carried			
5. Quality of outside sales personnel			
6. Quality of inside sales personnel			
7. Availability of products			
8. Delivery reliability			
9. Ability to follow up on complaints			
10. Quality of service			
11. Financial strength			
12. Size of firm			
13.			
14.			
15.			

Use your own judgment and the judgment of others within your firm, or ask a sample of customers representing each appropriate segment. Your criteria may be more specific and detailed than the examples we have provided.

Based upon this exercise, you should start to see the differences, if any, among your key segments. You will use this information in later chapters when you evaluate your competition and your market offerings.

When Do They Buy?

This information is necessary to plan sales calls, as well as to develop timely marketing support programs. Is the purchase a durable good, such as a piece of capital equipment? Is it a consumable, such as maintenance, repair, and operating (MRO) items? Is it a seasonal purchase? What is the order cycle?

These questions address the issue of timing. The buying cycle directly affects your selling cycle. For example, with capital goods, the selling cycle will be very long, and with many MRO products, the cycle will be short.

How Do They Buy?

How customers buy is a very important question that you must answer if you are to function as a nonmanipulative seller. The methods and processes that your customer utilizes to arrive at a purchase must be well defined in your mind. You cannot treat buyers as they wish to be treated if you do not have this knowledge. The basic structure of your selling strategy is influenced greatly by the answer to this question.

Buying Influences
Most business organizations are influenced by at least four forces:

1. Environmental: The economic, technological, political/legal, and competitive factors.
2. Organizational: The structure and organization of

the procurement function, along with the personality and culture of the firm.

3. Group: The composition of the buying centers, the decision criteria, the rules of behavior, and the risk involved.
4. Individual: The specific agenda and personality style of the individuals who constitute the buying center.

You must understand and incorporate each of these four levels into your sales approach to each segment and to firms within each segment.

Buying Process

There are several models of the general buying sequence in most organizations, but the formulation by Robinson, Faris, and Wind is widely accepted and helpful for field sellers. They specify an eight-phase sequence:

BUY PHASES	
1.	Anticipation or recognition of a problem (need)
2.	Determination of characteristics and quantity of needed item
3.	Description of characteristics and quantity of needed items
4.	Search for and qualification of potential sources
5.	Acquisition and analysis of proposals
6.	Evaluation of proposals and selection of suppliers
7.	Selection of order routine
8.	Performance feedback and evaluation

P. J. Robinson, C. W. Faris, and Yoram Wind, *Industrial Buying and Creative Marketing* (Boston: Allyn and Bacon, Inc., 1967).

This is a well-documented sequence. It behooves the seller to know what takes place at each step, who is involved, what is important, and how the seller can influence the process to the mutual advantage of both buyer and seller.

Buying Situations

A second component of the Robinson, Faris, and Wind model is labeled the buying situation. We will use both the buying phases and buying situations in chapter 8 when we discuss key account selling.

The *new task* is a situation in which the buying firm is going through extensive problem solving. The buyers lack well-defined criteria for evaluating products and vendors and any strong predisposition toward a particular solution. Any alternative is sufficiently different to require changes in the buyer's internal systems, such as manufacturing, inventory control, or finance.

The *straight rebuy* is basically routine response behavior. There are well-defined criteria on products and vendors. Automatic reordering systems are in place, and source loyalty is

Figure 5-3

TYPES OF BUYING SITUATIONS

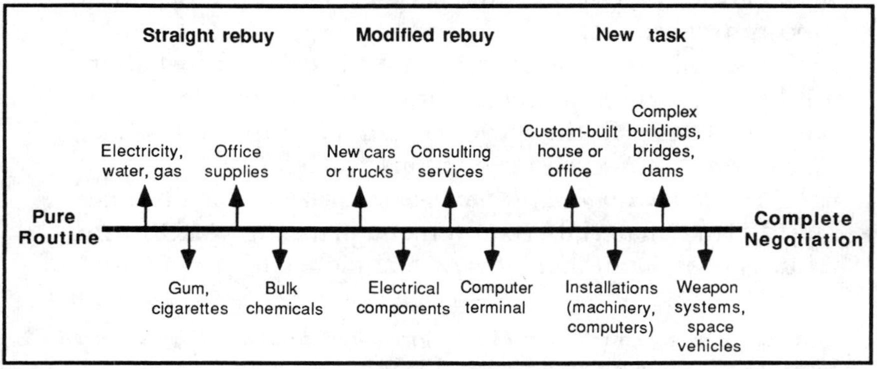

Marketing Principles, 3d ed. by Ben M. Enis. Copyright © 1980 Scott, Foresman and Company.

high. There is little need for information. The relationship is usually controlled by the purchasing agent.

The *modified rebuy* is a situation that is new, but similar enough to previous buys to be handled under existing systems and criteria. There may be some confusion as to which vendors can fit the needs. The numbers of participants may increase and gravitate up in the buying organization.

Some examples of buying situations are shown in Figure 5-3.

Using this information you can better understand your selling tasks. Your strategies will also depend on whether you are currently the supplier (in supplier) or not (out supplier). Figure 5-4 identifies some sales strategies for each.

Analytical Tools

There are some key tools that industrial buyers use to make their purchasing decisions. Spend some time understanding these analytical frameworks to understand better how you will be judged but also because they can be used as selling tools. A brief overview of some of these tools is presented here:*

> *Life cycle costing* considers the economic useful life of a product to a particular customer and then determines all of the costs that will be incurred over that life cycle. Categories of cost are initial costs, start-up costs, and postpurchase costs.
>
> *Value analysis* is the organized study of a product after it has been developed to identify unnecessary costs and to determine if the product can be improved while achieving desired cost reductions.
>
> *New purchasing and production systems.* Just-in-time (JIT) and materials requirement planning (MRP) are but two of a number of new techniques for improving

* Excerpt as specified from M.H. Morris, *Industrial and Organizational Marketing* (Columbus, Ohio: Merrill, 1988).

Figure 5-4

SELLING TASK ANALYSIS

| Buying Situtation | SUPPLIER STATUS | | Selling Task Summary |
	In Supplier	Out Supplier	
New Task	Monitor changing or emerging purchasing needs in organization. Isolate specific needs. If possible, participate actively in early phases of buying process by supplying information and technical advice.	Isolate specific needs. If possible, participate actively in early phases of buying process by supplying information and technical advice.	• Extensive Problem Solving • Consultative Selling
Straight Rebuy	Reinforce buyer-seller relationship by meeting organization's expectations. Be alert and responsive to changing needs of customer.	Convince organization that the potential benefits of reexamining requirements and suppliers exceed the costs. Attempt to gain a position on organization's perferred list of suppliers even as a second or third choice.	• Relationship Building or Reinforcing
Modified Rebuy	Act immediately to remedy problems with customer. Reexamine and respond to customer needs.	Define and respond to the organization's problem with existing supplier. Encourage organization to sample altenrative offerings.	• Limited Problem Solving • Network others in buying organization

Marketing Science Institute Series, Patrick J. Robinson, Charles W. Faris, and Yoram Wind, *Industrial Buying and Creative Marketing* (Boston: Allyn and Bacon, Inc., 1967), with modification.

efficiencies and lowering costs in purchasing, inventory control, and production. Other new production/operation systems, all made possible through advances in computer software, include manufacturing resource planning (MRP II), optimized production technology (OPT), distribution resource planning (DRP), and flexible manufacturing systems (FMS). As industrial customers adopt these systems, there are important implications for the marketer. Some possibilities include:

1. Closer, longer-term relationships between buyers and sellers, leading to more source loyalty and the use of fewer sources;
2. A change in the power relationship between buyer and seller, initially in favor of the buyer;
3. A greater emphasis on company attributes, and less on product attributes, when making sales;
4. Higher costs of products to the marketer but stable prices;
5. More complex price setting;
6. Greater emphasis on company attributes, and less on product attributes, when making sales;
7. Changes in the salesperson's role, with more stress on servicing and consulting activities;
8. Shorter, more direct distribution channels and higher logistical service levels;
9. A reliance on production scheduling patterns, service requirements, and geographic location, market segmentation, and target group selection.

General Trends in How Organizations Buy
The overall trends in purchasing and procurement are summarized in Figure 5-5.

Figure 5-5

CHANGING DIRECTIONS OF BUYER-SELLER RELATIONSHIPS

Trend in Purchasing/Procurement	Required Adaption by Industrial Marketer
Increased status and authority of purchasing managers in the organization.	Expand authority of industrial salesperson and utilize more sophisticated selling approaches.
Increased use of value analysis procedures by purchasing organizations.	Opportunity for creative applications of the same technique as a selling tool (for example, recommending cost-saving changes in the design of a component part).
Consolidation of purchasing, transportation, traffic, inventory control, and other departments into a materials management department.	More careful synchronization of selling distribution activities (for example, order processing, inventory control, transportation) to meet customer requirements.
Increased popularity and adoption of kan-ban(just-in-time) inventory control concepts by purchasing managers.	Improve logistical performance level (for example, delivery readability) in order to match the production requirements of customers.
Centralization of procurement at the headquarters level to consolidate purchasing power for geographically separated manufacturing facilities.	Learn to meet the special needs and selling requirements of these large national accounts.
Increased use of computer technology by purchasing organizations.	Increased need for knowledge of cost analysis and how computer technology can be used as a selling tool.

Reprinted by permission of the publisher from Michael D. Hutt & Thomas W. Speh, *Industrial Marketing Management,* p. 61. Copyright © 1985 by Elsevier Science Publishing Company, Inc.

Who Does the Buying?

Who are the participants in the buying? What role do they play? What criteria do they use to judge the offer? What must the seller do to adapt to different answers to these questions?

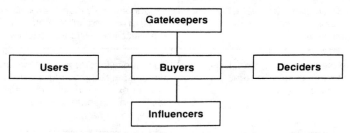

The *buying center* is defined as all individuals and groups participating in the buying decision process, either formally or informally. What does the buying center look like in terms of the participants?

Figure 5-6 defines the roles that each participant in the buying center plays. Different titles perform different roles or several roles at the same time.

The number of different individuals who play the various roles, as well as the organizational titles of the players, makes a big difference. For example, in straight rebuys and modified rebuys (with low risk) the typical interaction between the buyer and seller might be depicted as:

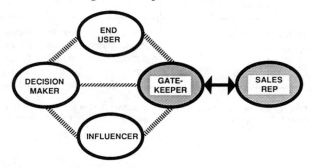

Reprinted by permission from John Barrett, "Why Major Account Selling Works," *Industrial Marketing Management,* Vol. 15, 63–73 (Copyright by Elsevier Publishing Company, 1986).

Figure 5-6

BUYING CENTER ROLES DEFINED

Role	Description
Users	As the role name implies, these are the personnel who will be using the product in question. Users may have anywhere from inconsequential to an extremely important influence on the purchase decision. In some cases, the users initiate the purchase by requesting the product. They may even develop the product specifications.
Gatekeepers	Gatekeepers control information to be reviewed by other members of the buying center. The control of information may be in terms of disseminating printed information or advertisements or through controlling which salesperson will speak to which individuals in the buying center. To illustrate, the purchasing agent might perform this screening role by opening the gate to the buying center for some sales personnel and closing it to others.
Influencers	These individuals affect the purchasing decision by supplying information for the evaluation of alternatives or by setting buying specifications. Typically, technical personnel, such as engineers, quality control personnel, and research and development personnel are significant influences on the purchase decision. Sometimes, individuals outside the buying organization can assume this role (e.g., an engineering consultant or an architect who writes very tight building specifications).
Deciders	Deciders are the individuals who actually make the buying decision, whether or not they have the formal authority to do so. The identity of the decider is the most difficult role to determine: buyers may have formal authority to buy, but the president of the firm may actually make the decision. A decider could be a design engineer who develops a set of specifications that only one vendor can meet.
Buyers	The buyer has formal authority for selecting the supplier and implementing all procedures connected with securing the product. The power of the buyer is often usurped by more powerful members of the organization. Often the buyer's role is assumed by the purchasing agent, who executes the clerical functions associated with a purchase order.

The purchasing agent will function as the gatekeeper, influencer, and, more than likely, the decision maker.

For a new task, a situation in which the risk is considerable, the buyer-seller interaction might be:

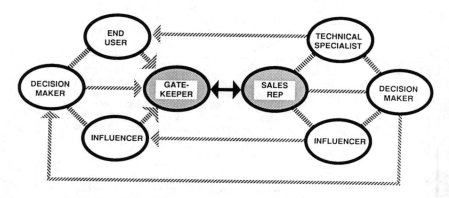

Reprinted by permission from John Barrett, "Why Major Account Selling Works," *Industrial Marketing Management,* Vol. 15, 63–73 (Copyright by Elsevier Publishing Company, 1986).

The seller is coordinating a sales team calling on a buying center. This team selling is becoming more common for several reasons:*

1. The Gatekeeper may not allow salespeople to meet the engineers, users, and others who are part of the buying center.

2. Often in geographic, product, or customer sales organizations, the seller has many customers and prospects to call on, making it difficult to allocate the time needed to penetrate the account.

* Reprinted by permission of the publisher from John Barrett, "Why Major Account Selling Works," *Industrial Marketing Management,* Vol. 15, 63–73 (copyright by Elsevier Publishing Company, 1986).

3. The seller must be able to "style-flex" to adapt to the background, values, and expectations of each member. This requires extensive knowledge, training, and time.

4. The Users/Influencers may be in other locations outside the seller's territory, making interaction physically impossible.

5. Where the selling company has a varied product line, the seller must be skilled in all areas to be able to satisfy the total needs of the account. The danger here is becoming a jack of all trades, master of none and losing credibility.

6. The background, perceptions, and personality of the seller may not blend well with all members of the buying center at all times of the buying process, creating unnecessary conflict between buyer and seller.

Who Else Can They Buy From?

Detailed competitive analysis is addressed in chapter 6. Our purpose at this stage is to determine who you must protect your Stars from and who you might want to go head to head with on accounts targeted in your Question Mark category. For the most part, competitive threats in your Cash Cow segments are minimal as long as you continue to perform. Most of your Cash Cow accounts will be in the straight rebuy situation. The key here is not to miss a change in purchase criteria and miss a new opportunity or give your competition a foot in the door. Worksheet 5-4 provides a format for identifying your key competitors.

Worksheet 5-4 (part 1)

KEY COMPETITORS: STAR AND QUESTION MARK CATEGORIES

	Segment Name			
STARS	A.	B.	C.	D.
COMPETITOR	NAMES OF KEY ACCOUNTS			
1._____				
2._____				
3._____				
4._____				

	Segment Name			
QUESTION MARKS	A.	B.	C.	D.
COMPETITOR	NAMES OF KEY ACCOUNTS			
1._____				
2._____				
3._____				
4._____				

How Do they Obtain Information?

In your targeted segments, how do buyers and participants in buying centers prefer to obtain their purchasing information? Are the preferred sources of information different across the various segments that you are selling? This datum will allow you to develop a more efficient approach to these segments. Use Worksheet 5-5 to collect this data.

Worksheet 5-5

CUSTOMER COMMUNICATION

INFORMATION SOURCE	TARGET MARKET SEGMENT				
	1.	2.	3.	4.	5.
1. Catalogs					
Comments:					
1. Catalogs					
Comments:					
1. Catalogs					
Comments:					
2. Price Lists					
Comments:					
3. Newspaper Ads					
Comments:					

93

Worksheet 5-5 (continued)

CUSTOMER COMMUNICATION

4. Radio Advertising Comments:					
5. Direct Mail Promo Comments:					
6. Inside Salespeople Comments:					
7. Outside Salespeople Comments:					
8. Comments:					
9. Comments:					
10. Comments:					

6

Selling against Competition

An important part of your territory planning is an assessment of your competition. We started some of this analysis in Chapter 4, but we need greater detail. In a survey published by *Training Magazine* some years ago, sales managers were asked about the biggest problems they have with their sales force. First on the list: they didn't prospect very well. And second: their salespeople didn't know enough about the competition. Just knowing about your competition will catapult you ahead of most other salespeople.

Types of Competitors

You have two types of competitors: direct and indirect. Direct competitors are people in the same business as you. They are basically going after the same customer dollars you are. Indirect competitors are not so easy to identify. Indirect competitors are alternative products that do not seem to be substitutes for your product offering. For example, your customer may decide to go with a service bureau to handle payroll as opposed to buying the computer from you, or he or she may simply decide to hire another accounting clerk to do the job. These different forms of competition compete for the same budget dollars.

You can't go around trying to identify every potential competitor in the marketplace and develop a file on their strengths and weaknesses. That would be impractical. But you can develop an awareness of your competitors that will keep you on your selling toes.

To identify your indirect competitors, give some thought to the nature of your product. Is it essential or a luxury? Does the customer have to get it somewhere, or could he or she get along well without it? The more essential it is, the fewer indirect competitors you'll have. The more discretionary it is, the more vulnerable you are to other tempting products on the market.

Let's focus more on the visible opponents—your direct competition. How do you stack up against them? You'll find very few products with no direct competition. An important part of your territory analysis is the evaluation of competitors. You want to identify all those who have a significant influence on the market segments you are interested in. Analyze their share of the market. Figure out their strengths and weaknesses. Where are they headed in the future?

Information Sources

Where do you go for these trade secrets?

You certainly don't want to do anything unethical or illegal. We're not talking about cloak-and-dagger intrigue and espionage. You don't have to go undercover to find valuable market intelligence. You will find that 70 to 90 percent of the data you need on your competition is available to the public.

For instance, a local public library is an obvious source to start with. Or you can try libraries of business schools. The federal government provides an amazing fountain of information. There are entire government staffs devoted to studying specific industries, and if you find the right people, they are generally very helpful. We recommend getting in touch with your state's department of economic development, which has information about local businesses. You might refer to the Census Bureau's booklet, *Current Industrial Reports.* It contains up-to-date information on about 40 percent of all manufacturing in the United States. The booklet has statistics on production, inventories, and orders of about 5,000 companies.

Gathering corporate intelligence can be very easy. Go to trade shows. There's a wealth of information about your competition just waiting for you. At these trade shows, a normally secretive company will load you down with brochures and demonstrate its new products all day long, so take advantage. Try them out and compare.

Check the classified ads. When a company advertises job openings, you will know it is expanding or changing in some other way. Subscribe to commercial data bases, which can direct you to articles about the companies you're interested in.

Trade information with business associates. Your informal contacts and relationships in the field will pass the word through the grapevine before it becomes official. Rumors spread quickly, and sometimes getting the word early gives you enough time to revise your game plan. Rumors are often distorted, but there's often a lot of truth to them. If used wisely, they can give you insights into the attitudes and opinions of and toward your competitors.

The more you know about your competition's plans—to release a new product, for instance—the better prepared you can be. You might find out that your competitor is planning a fall sales campaign. It is going to marshal all its resources to put a big push on special prices and special offers. If you know that in advance, you can prepare to compete. Otherwise you get caught short. Pay attention to what your customers tell you about the competition. When they make a comment, ask a question. Don't probe in the areas that are none of your business, but certainly pick up on the messages that are there for you.

Your customer could say, "I understand that there's a better deal coming along." You ask, "What makes you think that way?" They return, "Oh, you know; there are some other companies out there that have some other stuff." You might then take an indirect approach, backing off a little bit instead of probing in an intimidating way: "Well, every year each of the companies looks at the marketplace and lays out plans. They have certain products they push and certain products they don't push. What do you feel you're going to need? What would you be most willing to buy in the next quarter? Who else offers those products?" Your customer might say, "Well, I've seen the brochures on it." You reply, "Oh, really. Do you have a copy of that?" "Yeah," he says. "I've got one right here." You look at it and say, "Let's take a look and see how my product stacks up." And the two of you together wander through that brochure.

That brochure is common knowledge; it isn't privileged information. In the course of your fact-finding mission, the customer is telling you what your competitor has that is appealing. Or if the buyer chooses your product, he or she can tell you what edge you have over your competitors. It's to the customer's advantage to engage you in this conversation. As a good salesperson, you'll do what you can to make a better offer than the competition.

For you, the main thing is keep your antennas out. With a little imagination, you can get almost any kind of information.

Stay in touch with your company, and let everyone know you want all the facts on your competition. Make sure your sales manager knows you're interested in what's going on. Make sure what gets discussed in the marketing boardroom gets communicated to you.

The following are useful sources:

- *Standard & Poor's* Industry Surveys
- *Forbes Annual Report on Business*
- *Moody's Industrial Manual*
- *Dun & Bradstreet Reference Book of Corporate Management*
- *Standard & Poor's Corporate Record*
- *Encyclopedia of Business Information Sources*
- Periodicals
- Government publications from the U.S. Department of Commerce, U.S. Treasury Department (Internal Revenue Service), Bureau of Census, Bureau of Economic Analysis, and Department of Labor
- *Funk & Scott Index of Corporations and Industries*
- *Wall Street Transcript*
- Newspapers
- Trade journals
- Consulting firms
- Annual reports, stock prospectuses, stock performance guides
- Personal contacts
- Company's resources, other salespeople
- Trade associations
- Trade shows
- Commercial suppliers, such as Frost & Sullivan and Stanford Research Institute
- Academic institutions

Competitive Analysis

Identification

To evaluate your direct competitors, go back to our old friend, the product/market target matrix:

| THE MARKET-TARGET SEGMENT MIX | | | |
Market Target A	Market Target B	Market Target N	Horizontal Totals
			Grand Total

(Row labels, top to bottom: Product Line 1, Product Line 2, Product Line N, Vertical Totals. Left vertical label: THE PRODUCT MIX)

In each cell on the matrix, identify the three or four major competitors to your products. Use whatever criteria you feel are appropriate, but the primary piece of information must be their market share. Use worksheet 6-1 for this purpose.

Worksheet 6-1 will give you good insight into the competitive marketplace. Don't be too concerned about the exactness of the market-share numbers. This is a relative measure and serves to rank your primary competitors. Whether the market share is 28 percent or 35 percent is not critical. The "All Others" category is one that should be of interest to you if it accounts for a significant percentage of market potential. Perhaps you should be a bit more concerned about these smaller players. Perhaps you could capture some of their business.

Worksheet 6-1

COMPETITOR ANALYSIS: IDENTIFICATION

TARGET MARKET SEGMENT _____

Product Lines	Your Firm			Rival Firm's Estimated Market Shares				
	Potential Total Dollars Purchased	Sales Volume	Share of Market	1.	2.	3.	4.	5. All Others
A.								
B.								
C.								
TOTAL								
Trends ↑, ↓, or N.C.								

101

If you cannot fill out the required information, perhaps you really do not know your market. The worksheet is difficult to complete if you don't know your competition.

Relative Strengths

Simply knowing your competition is not enough. Their relative strengths and weaknesses are of vital importance as well. What do they bring to the party? How do they penetrate and maintain their accounts? Where are they vulnerable?

By identifying the attributes or purchase criteria in each segment and their measured importance by segment, you can judge each competitor according to the expectations of each segment. (The Appendix explains in more detail how to identify these attributes or purchase criteria and how to rate their importance by segment.) On Worksheet 6-2, compare your company and the competition to those selection criteria of importance in each segment. Rate your perception of the ability of your firm versus your primary competitors in terms of their strengths (strong, average, or poor) on each criterion.

Strategy Implications

Using the information you have just developed for your firm and for each major competitor, describe your relative strengths and weaknesses. Using our matrix format, you can summarize your findings segment by segment, firm by firm. On the vertical axis is the degree of importance of the selection criteria; on the horizontal is the strength of performance for each firm.

The matrix would then look like this:

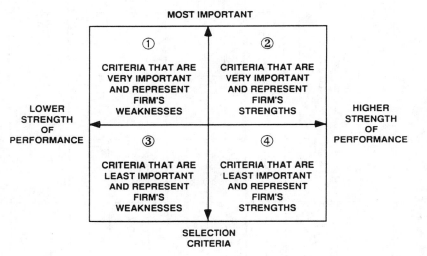

SELECTION
CRITERIA

MOST IMPORTANT

① CRITERIA THAT ARE VERY IMPORTANT AND REPRESENT FIRM'S WEAKNESSES

② CRITERIA THAT ARE VERY IMPORTANT AND REPRESENT FIRM'S STRENGTHS

LOWER STRENGTH OF PERFORMANCE

HIGHER STRENGTH OF PERFORMANCE

③ CRITERIA THAT ARE LEAST IMPORTANT AND REPRESENT FIRM'S WEAKNESSES

④ CRITERIA THAT ARE LEAST IMPORTANT AND REPRESENT FIRM'S STRENGTHS

SELECTION
CRITERIA

LEAST IMPORTANT

Cell 1: "Serious Problems"

Any criteria in this cell are serious weaknesses for your firm. You must work to improve these factors to have a competitive offering in this segment. If they cannot be improved, you must seriously reconsider your selection of this segment as a target. Any of your competitor's falling in this cell represent opportunities for your organization to attack and capitalize on.

Cell 2: "Keep Up the Good Work"

For both your firm and the competition, this cell represents strengths. More important, these are relative strengths that are appreciated by the segment's accounts.

Cell 3: "Needs Watching"

You should not be spending time or resources here. These factors may be part of a total offering that has

Worksheet 6-2

COMPETITIVE ANALYSIS: RELATIVE STRENGTHS

Target Market Segment _____

Selection Criteria or Attribute	IMPORTANCE 3 = Very Important 2 = Important 1 = Not Important	YOUR FIRM	RATINGS			
			COMPETITORS			
			1. ____	2. ____	3. ____	4. ____
1. General reputation						
2. Quality of products carried						
3. Range of products carried						
4. Prices of products carried						
5. Quality of outside sales personnel						
6. Quality of inside sales personnel						
7. Availability of products						
8. Delivery reliability						
9. Ability to follow up on complaints						
10. Quality of service						
11. Financial strength						
12. Size of firm						
13.						
14.						
15.						

RATINGS: 3 = Strong Performer   2 = Average Performer   1 = Poor Performer

some value, but they by no means make the difference. Make sure that your competitors are not educating this segment to increase the importance of these criteria. You should continue to monitor changes to keep abreast of this possibility.

Cell 4: "Why Bother?"

This segment does not value these criteria even though they represent strengths. Unless the importance of these criteria can be increased or there are other segments that value these things, they are phantom strengths. They do not give you any advantage, and you may turn off these accounts. Have you ever been approached by a seller who kept talking about features or benefits that were of little interest to you? You now understand this cell.

Use Worksheet 6-3 for each competitor in each of your target market segments.

From this exercise, you'll quickly see which areas need improving. You'll also recognize which areas to emphasize in your selling efforts. For example, if your company is strong on pricing but weak in delivery, do what you can to improve delivery and emphasize pricing as a selling point. By knowing which competitor is highest in customer service, you'll know whom to study.

Be objective. For example, as a salesperson for Ikegami Tsushinki, you sell video cameras to television stations, advertising agencies, educational institutions, hospitals, security firms, and home users—to name just a few. The competition is made up of companies like Sony, JVC, and Panasonic. Although Ikegami commands the biggest share of the broadcast market, it doesn't dominate the home market. It would not have many factors in cell 2 for this segment.

It's not enough simply to observe the standing of your company and its competitors. You have to find out *why* these standings are as they are. Then answer the next question:

Worksheet 6-3

COMPETITIVE ANALYSIS: STRATEGY IMPLICATIONS

Firm _____

Market Segment _____

SELECTION CRITERIA
MOST IMPORTANT

List factors that are important and represent firm's weaknesses.	List factors that are very important and represent firm's strengths.

Poor Performance ←→ **Excellent Performance**

List factors considered to be least important and represent firm's weaknesses.	List factors that are least important and are considered to be firm's strengths.

SELECTION CRITERIA
LEAST IMPORTANT

"How can these standings be changed so that my company gets a bigger share next year in the segments we would like to penetrate?"

After you've analyzed the various market segments, you will be sensitive to the factors that influence sales in each segment. Sony Corporation, for instance, would look at the fact that broadcasters will pay for a camera with the highest-quality picture, while a security firm will shop for reliability and the lowest unit price.

You may want to survey the businesses or industries within the market segments to determine how you and the competitors rate on each of these selection criteria.

Positioning

You have tried to assess the needs of your target markets and measure the potential for your products and services. You have taken a stab at comparing you and your primary competitors to the market needs. You have taken a look at the conditions that exist in the marketplace and tried to figure out how to use them to your advantage. It may seem like expensive, time-consuming work. After all, the information you gather will soon be out of date. But just think of the cost of not understanding what you're up against.

Having identified the factors most important to each market segment in their decision to purchase a product or service like yours, you can answer some interesting questions. How important is your company's reputation to your different markets? How important are your pricing, delivery, and quality? How do your customer service and financial strength affect the buying decisions made in each of your market segments?

This analysis will help steer you toward the markets in which you can capitalize on the strengths of your company and product. For example, if you sell an expensive but reliable copying machine, you want to know which market segment values reliability over purchase price. In your research you might find that banks and stationers buy those brands that are reliable but that law firms favor the lower price for the less reliable machines.

The question that must be answered at this point is, "Why should my target segments buy from me instead of from my competition?"

Your product and firm are perceived by various buyers as having a certain personality or position as compared to your competitors. Two classic illustrations of positioning, which appear in Al Ries and Jack Trout's book, *Positioning—The Battle for Our Mind*, are 7-Up as the "Uncola" and Avis as number two but trying harder.

Positioning is much broader than just promotion. The value of positioning is that it integrates several of the elements of your total offering. You can alter your offering's position in the mind of your customers.

A number of elements go into your market position, including:

- Product (features, breadth of line, packaging, etc.)
- Advertising (media, appeals, etc.)
- Pricing (list, discounts, etc.)
- Availability (minimum order quantity, ease of purchase, etc.)
- Sales force (order takers, consultative sellers, etc.)
- Customer service (training, responsiveness, etc.)
- R&D (innovativeness, intuitiveness, etc.)
- Market research (capabilities, creativeness, etc.)
- Manufacturing (quality, flexibility, etc.)
- Distribution (promptness, reliability, etc.)
- Technical service (availability, expertise, etc.)
- Engineering support (availability, expertise, etc.)
- Purchasing (quality, control, etc.)
- Finance (flexibility, responsiveness, etc.)
- Installation (availability, skills, etc.)

Worksheet 6-4

COMPETITIVE ANALYSIS: POSITIONING

Product Line _____   Market Segment _____

| POSITIONING STRATEGY |
| (Benefits, Advantages, Features) |

_____

_____

_____

_____

_____

_____

_____

_____

COMPONENTS

Product

_____

_____

_____

Pricing

_____

_____

_____

Promotion

_____

_____

_____

Distribution

_____

_____

_____

**Internal
Support**

_____

_____

_____

For each of your target market segments, you and your firm, based on all previous analyses, should develop a statement of your positioning strategy.

An example of the positioning for Deborah's firm, offering software to the financial segment, might be: "In this financial segment, we are positioned as the most creative and reliable provider of software programs; we increase operating efficiency and operating margins through extensive technical support, trained consultative sellers, and R&D that is competent in financial applications." There may be several additional elements addressing, for example, pricing or distribution.

Use Worksheet 6-4 to develop an overview of your positioning strategy for each product line in each appropriate market segment. Look at the various elements and develop insight into the benefits and features relationships. Keep in mind the analysis that you did on Worksheet 6-3.

You have now developed a comprehensive listing of your competitive strengths and weaknesses. But you should constantly update your information. Competitors have a way of coming and going and changing their strategies. Keep abreast of your marketplace for both your short-run selling strategies and for the longer-term directions and strategies of your firm and others.

7

Developing the Territory Plan

THE cartoon on page 112 appeared on a sales promotion piece from Economic Information System, a research firm. It serves to illustrate the importance of territory planning very well. Obviously Vernon has no idea of the value of his time or of the need to generate gross profit margin dollars to cover at least the cost of the sales call. He probably spent $5,000 to generate an order for $500 at 20 percent gross margin. Sadly, many salespeople fall into this same trap—an order for the sake of an order. Unless Vernon's breakthrough represents a sale to a strategic account that has long-term implications, this effort leaves much to be desired. Where else could Vernon have been investing his time? What other opportunities exist in his market? Could this sale have been made by a less costly form of sales—inside reps or telemarketing?

You must program your efforts to take advantage of your scarcest resource—selling time. Time is an interesting commodity. You cannot inventory it. When it becomes available, it must be used. This leads salespeople to the philosophy that making a call—any call—is better than not making one. It would make more sense to generate as many sales calls as is appropriate but to have planned the calls to maximize the return, that is, to work smarter rather than harder.

"THE BREAKTHROUGH"

Your territory plan will encompass the following areas:

- Territory opportunities and problems
- Territory objectives
- Territory strategy
- Territory tactics
- Territory control

You have done quite a bit of this analysis already in previous chapters. Your objective here is to bring this analysis and direction to the street. Your job in this chapter is to move from the segments to the individual accounts within each of those targeted segments.

Territory Opportunities and Problems

Using the information from Chapters 4, 5, and 6, you should be able to identify the major opportunities and problems in your territory. Opportunities and problems can arise from both inside and outside the company. Environmental and market influences can affect sales as much as company policies, products, or services. Factors in the market that may cause increased opportunities include changes in consumer demand, fads, increased affluence due to social mobility, and the increased impact of technology. In fact, technology is such a strong influence on products that manufacturers estimate that more than half of their existing products have been on the market for fewer than five years.

Opportunities that stem from your company are the easiest to define and take advantage of. In your competitive analysis, you should have listed those strengths that put your company and its products ahead of your competitors. Your company can also create opportunities through introducing new products or improving old ones. New features and benefits often create renewed interest and sales. Promotional specials accomplish the same purpose.

Every market segment and company has problems. There's no denying that some problems in the field were created by the company. Sometimes poor management causes the company's image to be less than ideal. Often a salesperson will start working for a company that has changed ownership and needs to overcome a bad reputation. This adds another challenge to the task of selling. A new reputation is built through the sales force and service, so your role is essential.

Other influences from outside the company can cause problems. Unfavorable market trends can shift business away from you. Customers can be very fickle; a change in technology or fads may trigger them to switch to another company. Although changing fads can create opportunities, they can also dry up a market. Stiff competition can cause problems, and it's tough on a salesperson. There's no denying that some companies dominate a market segment. You need to make an extra effort to compete with them.

Isolate the problems and opportunities and note ways for dealing with them. You cannot do this just once, however. Being aware of changes is a key part of being a successful salesperson. Use the concepts and formats in the previous chapters at least once a year.

Territory Objectives

Setting objectives is the next step in managing your territory. The objectives you create should flow directly from your situation analysis, as well as your personal and organizational priorities. Naturally, these goals will be aimed at overcoming problems and exploiting opportunities.

There are several other reasons for setting territory objectives. First, they serve as an incentive to motivate you. Only when you are challenged sufficiently will you seek new performance levels and strive toward loftier goals. Second, objectives define and control your activities. They take the randomness out of your calls by creating priorities. Objectives suggest action to be taken. Finally, concrete objectives give you something by which to evaluate your performance.

The objectives you set for your territory should include all accounts, market segments, products and services, and promotional and travel expenses. Some examples of territory objectives are:

1. Increasing the dollar volume for entire territory.
2. Increasing the percentage in volume over last year by a certain percentage range.
3. Increasing sales of certain products by certain amounts.
4. Increasing overall sales or specific product sales in particular market segments.
5. Reducing by a certain percentage overhead expenses for the entire territory.
6. Adding specific market segments to the overall sales effort.
7. Increasing the number of new accounts over last year by a certain percentage.
8. Increasing total dollar sales per customer.
9. Upgrading a certain percentage of C accounts to B's and B accounts to A's.
10. Seeing a certain number of prospects per week and turning a certain percentage of them into accounts.
11. Reducing the cost of sales calls by a certain percentage.
12. Increasing the ratio of actual sales to sales calls.
13. Adding a certain number of qualified prospects to your files per month or year.

We could go on and on listing objectives. The point is that your objectives will have to custom fit your customers, products and services, market segments, and territory. Your choice of objectives will make the difference between effective and ineffective management and sales in your territory.

Territory Strategy

Everything that you do requires a strategy. Each of your territory objectives should have a strategy—a "how-to." In order to develop these strategies, you will have to identify and analyze individual accounts in your territory, evaluate their potential, classify them according to their attractiveness, set objectives, and then decide when and how to call on them, how many to call on, and with what frequency. You will also have to identify any required support programs or which other forms of selling can better serve some of the accounts. Figure 7-1 depicts the strategy portion of your plan. A good portion of this chapter focuses on this concept.

Account Analysis

The first step in developing your territory strategy is to do a complete audit of your account base. A territory is a marketing concept, not a geographic one. Many salespeople lose sight of this distinction and work by geography, not potential. The geographic territory is used only to distinguish your area of responsibility from that of another seller. Your territory should be construed as a portion of your firm's market potential that has been assigned to you for care and feeding. Some sellers work the entire geography in their territory. That makes sense only if all parts of your market are equally attractive. When you are in one part of your market or in a specific account, you cannot be someplace else. Working your territory is a system of trade-offs based on the various accounts' attractiveness and your chances of selling them. The logic of the audit is depicted in Figure 7-2.

Figure 7-1

TERRITORY STRATEGY

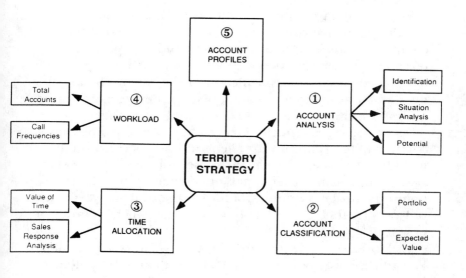

Figure 7-2

AUDIT LOGIC

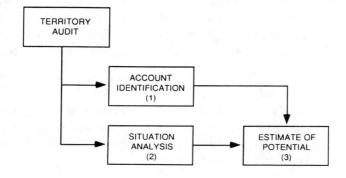

Account Identification

Now that you have some idea of the market segments you will go after, you need to learn more about the individual accounts. List all the major customers and prospects in your territory for each market segment. By now you have done enough research to have uncovered the major clients. You may have to stretch your imagination and devote more time to finding specific prospects. Take the time to do this.

As we will discuss in Chapter 9, your need for prospects is continual. To organize your client and prospect list, we have included Worksheet 7-1 for you to use. Fill out a worksheet for every product and every market segment you sell. At this point, the order is unimportant. After you've analyzed each prospect further, go back and list your customers in order of priority.

In Worksheet 7-1, just identify the accounts at this time. You will eventually have to determine their sales potential. Use your current sales records for the existing accounts. See the list on page 177 for some sources of information that you can use to identify prospects.

Situation Analysis

Just as you evaluated the various segments in Chapter 4, you should use the same logic on these individual accounts. To the best of your knowledge, assess the account's viability. This situation analysis is a qualifying step in determining the estimated potential of the account. In order to be selective in your investment of selling time, you must know the account's attractiveness in relation to other accounts in your territory.

Estimate of Potential

Do not be overly concerned about the accuracy of this estimate. As long as you are using the same methodology on all of the accounts, your estimate of potential will be correct in a relative sense, if not in absolute terms.

Worksheet 7-1

ACCOUNT IDENTIFICATION

Market Segment _____   Product Line_____

Existing Customers / Clients	**Prospects**

You can use the rates of usage in the Appendix to estimate the potential of prospects and to check the total potential of your existing accounts. Use Worksheet 7-2 to organize your thinking. You may have several product lines for each account. Add all of the potentials for each product line to obtain the total account potential. On your existing accounts, you will have this information readily available.

For prospects, the required information is more difficult to obtain. Some research using the telephone may be appropriate. You might also estimate the potential for prospective accounts by comparing them to similar accounts that you may have already sold.

Be selective in identifying prospects. Stay within the segments you have categorized as Stars. Since these are the segments in which you have strengths and the segments are growing, the likelihood of identifying better prospects is greater in this category.

Account Classification

You've spent hours researching and analyzing, but what has it all been for? In one word—*priorities*! It takes knowledge to decide what to do and when to do it, or, in your case, who to call on and when. The analysis of each account and prospect will show you in hard figures which calls are worth your time and effort and which are not. Pareto's 80-20 principle states that 20 percent of your accounts constitute 80 percent of your total sales. The sales expenses for each of these key accounts are not much greater than for the smaller, less profitable accounts. You must identify and cater to them and make them grow.

To set your priorities, look at your customers from two points of view. First, what will each account contribute to your overall sales and profits? Second, what is the time investment necessary to cover that account and realize the profit poten-

Worksheet 7-2

ESTIMATION OF ACCOUNT POTENTIAL

(1) ACCOUNT	(2) S. I. C.	(3) PRODUCT LINES	(4) RATE OF USAGE	(5) NO. OF EMPLOYEES	(4 X 5) ACCOUNT POTENTIAL
1.					
2.					
3.					
4.					
5.					
6.					
7.					
8.					
9.					
10.					
11.					
12.					
13.					
14.					
15.					
16.					
17.					
18.					
19.					
20.					
21.					
22.					
23.					
24.					
25.					

• Use rate developed in the Appendix

• Multiply Column 4 and Column 5 and sum
for all products for a given account
OR
use your best estimate of account potential
if you have not used the Appendix.

121

tial? An important part of this second analysis is to determine the worth of your time on an hourly basis. The profitability of an account can be determined only if you have an idea of the overhead costs of your product, and the cost includes your time as a salesperson.

There are two methods for classifying your accounts. Both force you to make some judgments regarding the value of the account to you. This index of attractiveness becomes the basis for classifying your accounts into A, B, and C categories. The A accounts are most attractive, then the B, then the C.

Porter Henry, in his audio program *Investing Your Sales Time for Maximum Return,* discusses a principle he refers to as IFUM: the Important Few, the Unimportant Many. As you can see from Figure 7-3, your A accounts are truly important.

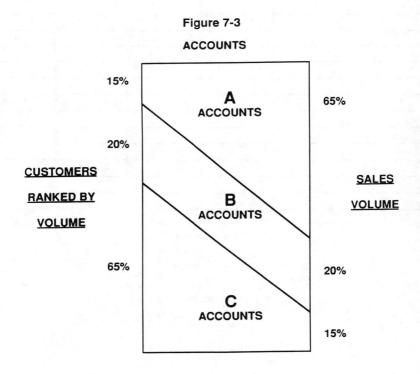

Figure 7-3

ACCOUNTS

CUSTOMERS RANKED BY VOLUME

SALES VOLUME

The two methods that you might use for this process are *expected value* and *account portfolio analysis*.

Expected Value
The formula for calculating the expected value for your prospective accounts is:

$$EV = MP \times ES \times P$$
where
EV = Expected Value
MP = Market Potential of the prospect
ES = Your Expected Share of this potential
P = The Probability of your getting the expected share

To illustrate, suppose that John has identified a prospect in the financial segment for software products. This account, Ames-Acme Savings and Loan, has eighty employees at this location. The consumption rate, which is the average annual purchase per employee, for this segment for software is $150. Therefore, using our formula:

$$\text{Ames-Acme } EV = MP \times ES \times P$$
$$MP \rightarrow \text{number of employees} \times \text{consumption rate}$$
$$80 \times \$150 = \$12,000.$$

John has had some contact with this type of account and feels that it will be receptive to his selling efforts. He feels that they will give him an initial trial order of 20 percent of their needs. Therefore:

$$EV = \$12,000 \times .20 \times P.$$

Based on similar accounts and his selling experience with them, John feels that there is an excellent probability of obtaining this share of the accounts business. Therefore:

$$EV = \$12{,}000 \times .2 \times P$$
$$P = 20\% = \text{fair chance}$$
$$50\% = \text{average chance}$$
$$80\% = \text{excellent chance}$$

The expected value of this account is:

$$EV = \$12{,}000 \times .2 \times .8$$
$$= \$1{,}920$$

What is this number? It is a simple index. If John carried out the same calculation on all of his accounts (existing and prospects) and then ranked them from the highest expected value to the lowest, the top 10 percent would be his A accounts. The next 30 percent would be the B accounts, and the remaining 60 percent would be C accounts.

Suppose John had 200 accounts: 120 on the books and 80 prospects. Accounts 1 to 20 would be the A, 21 to 81 the B, and 82 through 200 the C accounts.

Use Worksheet 7-3 to conduct a similar analysis on your prospects. The calculation must be modified slightly for your existing accounts. Since you already have a base of business on these existing accounts, you have to be concerned only about any additional volume on the account that you are not obtaining. The formula for your existing accounts is:

$$EV = CB + (AV \times P)$$

where:

CB = Current Base of business
AV = Additional Volume
P = Probability of capturing the additional volume

For example, John has sold Jones Commercial Bank $10,000 worth of software products each year for the past four years. There is the potential for $16,000 worth of sales to this account annually. The additional volume (AV) is $16,000 minus $10,000. Therefore:

$$EV = \$10{,}000 + (\$6{,}000 \times P).$$

Worksheet 7-3

EXPECTED VALUE: PROSPECTS

PROSPECT	MARKET POTENTIAL	ESTIMATED SHARE	PROBABILITY	EXPECTED VALUE	CATEGORY

PROBABILITY   .2 Fair
                   .5 Average
                   .8 Excellent

125

Although this volume is rather sizable, Jones is very reluctant to give all of its software business to a single vendor. John therefore feels that its policy of dual sourcing will prevent him from capturing the additional volume. Therefore:

$$EV = \$10,000 + (\$6,000 \times .2)$$
$$= \$10,000 + \$1,200$$
$$= \$11,200$$

What exactly does this number mean? Since John has used the same logic on all the accounts, it simply means that the higher the number is, the more attractive the account is. John still has to work the account and develop strategies and programs to get the job done. This classification procedure just helps to assign priorities.

Use Worksheet 7-4 to calculate an expected value for your existing accounts. Worksheet 7-5 is a summary of your account classification based upon the EV calculation.

Although this procedure is subjective, it is based on your best estimates. You often refer to your "gut" feeling. This procedure allows you to quantify your "gut" feeling and put it on paper.

You used gross sales dollars in this classification scheme. In many cases, it would be a better idea to use gross margin dollars as your measure of the accounts potential. Gross margin is defined as:

$$GM = GS - COS,$$

where:

GM = Gross Margin (in dollars)
GS = Gross Sales (in dollars)
COG = Cost of Goods sold (in dollars)

It is easier to obtain the gross margin percentage (GMP) for each of your product lines. The calculation then becomes:

$$GM = GS \times GMP$$

where:

$$GM = \text{Gross Margin (in dollars)}$$
$$GS = \text{Gross Sales (in dollars)}$$
$$GMP = \text{Gross Margin (percentage)}$$

Add these gross margin dollars for all the products that the account could buy. These gross margin dollars reflect the important dollars since the gross sales could be quite large but your firm would not be making much in the way of profit if you were not selling the higher-margin items or if you were forced to give price discounts on the sale. For example,

	Ames-Acme	**Jones**
Gross sales	$10,000	$20,000
COG	8,000	19,000
GM	$ 2,000	$ 1,000

Although Acme is only half the gross sales dollars, it is capable of generating twice as many gross margin dollars.

If possible, obtain the gross margin percentage for your products. If this is not available, use the gross sales dollars.

The second method of classifying accounts is slightly different and not so dependent on quantifying your judgments.

Account Portfolio Analysis
This approach is similar to the method that you used in chapter 4 to develop your segment portfolio. It considers the following two factors:

Account opportunity indicates how much the account needs your products and whether it is able to buy the products. Some of the factors used to determine the opportunity are account potential, growth rate, financial condition, profit margin, and reputation.

Strength of position indicates how strong you and your firm are in selling the account. Some of the factors used to determine your strength of position are relationships

Worksheet 7-4

EXPECTED VALUE: CURRENT ACCOUNTS

CUSTOMER/ ACCOUNT	REPEAT SALES	ADDITIONAL VOLUME	PROBABILITY	EXPECTED VALUE	CATEGORY

PROBABILITY   .2 Fair
               .5 Average
               .8 Excellent

Worksheet 7-5

ACCOUNT CLASSIFICATIONS

PRIORITY A ACCOUNTS

RANK	ACCOUNT

TOTAL POTENTIAL $ _____

% TOTAL POTENTIAL _____

PRIORITY B ACCOUNTS

RANK	ACCOUNT

TOTAL POTENTIAL $ _____

% TOTAL POTENTIAL _____

PRIORITY C ACCOUNTS

NUMBER OF ACCOUNTS _____

TOTAL POTENTIAL $ _____

% TOTAL POTENTIAL _____

with the account, past experience with the account, attitude of the account toward you and your firm, share of the account's business, and familiarity with key decision makers.

Using a simple rating procedure (which we will show you in a bit), you can classify your territory's accounts into the grid or portfolio seen in Figure 7-4. Segment 1 accounts constitute

Figure 7-4

ACCOUNT PORTFOLIO

STRENGTH OF POSITION

	Strong	Weak

High	**Segment 1**
	
	Attractiveness:
	  Accounts are very attractive since they offer high opportunity and sales organization has strong postion.
	
	Sales call strategy:
	  Accounts should receive a high level of sales calls since they are the sales organization's most attractive accounts.
		Segment 2
		
		Attractiveness:
		  Accounts are potentially attractive since they offer high opportunity, but sales organization currently has weak position with accounts.
		
		Sales call strategy:
		  Accounts should receive a high level of sales calls to strengthen the sales organization's position.

Low	**Segment 3**
	
	Attractiveness:
	  Accounts are somewhat attractive since sales organization has strong position, but future opportunity is limited.
	
	Sales call strategy:
	  Accounts should receive a moderate level of sales calls to maintain the current strength of the sales organization's position.
		Segment 4
		
		Attractiveness:
		  Accounts are very unattractive since they offer low opportunity and sales organization has weak position.
		
		Sales call strategy:
		  Accounts should receive a minimal level of sales calls and efforts made to eliminate or replace personal sales calls with telephone sales calls, direct mail, etc.

ACCOUNT OPPORTUNITY (row label, left side spanning High/Low)

Raymond W. LaForge, Clifford E. Young, and B. Curtis Hamm, "Increasing Sales Productivity Through Improved Sales Call Allocation Strategies," *Journal of Personal Selling and Sales Management,* Nov 83, pp. 53–59.

your A category, segment 2 your B accounts, segment 3 your C accounts, and segment 4 should probably not be handled by field sellers.

Worksheets 7-6, 7-7, and 7-8 should be used to build your account portfolio.

Worksheet 7-6 measures the account's opportunity. Use any criteria that you feel are important in qualifying an account in terms of its attractiveness to you. Some of the criteria that may be used are:

- Market position
- Growth rate of account's business
- Financial position of account
- Tenure of account
- Size of account

On Worksheet 7-6, list your accounts down the left-hand side and your evaluation criteria across the top. Now rate each account as either 4, 3, 2, or 1 based on your best estimate. Add these ratings to obtain a score for each account. You may need several of these worksheets to cover all of your territory.

In a similar fashion, use Worksheet 7-7 to develop a score for your strength of position on each account. Some examples of criteria:

- Previous experience with account
- Familiarity with account operations
- Relationships with decision makers at account
- Relationships with product users at account
- Attitude of account toward company
- Product distribution at account
- Shelf space at account

Now place each account in the portfolio that is Worksheet 7-8. Scale the two dimensions based on the numbers that you

Worksheet 7-6

ACCOUNT OPPORTUNITY

CRITERIA

ACCOUNT	1. _____	2. _____	3. _____	4. _____	5. _____	TOTAL
1.						
2.						
3.						
4.						
5.						
6.						
7.						
8.						
9.						
10.						
11.						
12.						
13.						
14.						
15.						
16.						
17.						
18.						
19.						
20.						
21.						
22.						
23.						
24.						
25.						

RATINGS: 4 Highly Favorable
3 Favorable
2 Unfavorable
1 Highly Unfavorable

Worksheet 7-7

STRENGTH OF POSITION

CRITERIA

ACCOUNTS	1. _____	2. _____	3. _____	4. _____	5. _____	TOTAL
1.						
2.						
3.						
4.						
5.						
6.						
7.						
8.						
9.						
10.						
11.						
12.						
13.						
14.						
15.						
16.						
17.						
18.						
19.						
20.						
21.						
22.						
23.						
24.						
25.						

RATINGS: 4 Very Strong
3 Strong
2 Weak
1 Very Weak

133

Worksheet 7-8

ACCOUNT PORTFOLIO

STRENGTH OF POSITION

	STRONG			WEAK		
H I G H						
A C C O U N T						
O P P O R T U N I T Y						
L O W						

134

developed in your ratings. The number system on Worksheet 7-8 is based on using five criteria on both dimensions. Therefore, the highest score is 20 and the lowest possible is 5. If you use more or fewer criteria, modify the scale. You are looking at a positioning system, not a mathematical concept. The numbers are only a tool to help you categorize your accounts.

Regardless of which method you choose, expected value or account portfolio analysis, you are now in a position to develop your call strategies in terms of your time allocation.

Time Allocation

The logical starting point in the deployment of your time is to get a better understanding of the value of your time in dollars. Then you can address the question: How do categories of accounts and individual accounts respond to various levels of sales effort?

Value of Time
The method of deriving your time's worth takes into consideration the direct costs accrued in your pursuit of an account. These costs include your salary, bonuses, commissions, travel expenses, and miscellaneous expenses. The formula is:

$$CPH = \frac{DC}{WH}$$

where:

CPH = Cost per Hour
DC = Direct Costs
WH = Working Hours

For example, let's say a salesperson's direct costs are:

Salary	$30,000
Commissions	10,000
Travel	10,000
Miscellaneous	5,000
Direct costs	$55,000

This is fairly typical because direct costs are approximately twice the salesperson's salary. To figure cost per hour (*CPH*), divide direct costs by 2,000 working hours based on forty hours per week for fifty weeks of the year (if your working hours differ from our figure, please use your own figures):

$$CPH = \frac{DC}{WH} = \frac{\$55,000}{2,000} = \$27.50/\text{hr.}$$

In this example, the salesperson's time is worth $27.50 per hour. This is not terribly accurate, however, because none of us is fully productive for forty hours a week. It's nice to think we're being paid while we eat lunch, but in reality it's just not so. It's much more accurate to assume that your "call hours" are the only productive hours in your day. To know the worth of your time during the sales call (and later to determine whether you're wasting time), you need to divide your direct costs by the number of call hours (*CH*) in a year rather than the total hours worked.

$$\text{Cost per Call Hour } (CPCH) = \frac{DC}{CH} = \frac{\$55,000}{800} = \$68.75/\text{hr.}$$

The cost per call hour is important to keep in mind so that you can aspire to earn more money per call hour than you cost your company so that you can be in the black rather than in the red or simply breaking even.

Now that you know what your time is worth per call hour, you can figure how much you have to sell in order to break even. In calculating your break-even volume, you must know the gross margin of your products. Let's use the case of a salesperson getting a product for one price and selling it for another. The difference will be the gross profit margin. The formula for calculating break-even volume is:

$$BEV = \frac{DC}{GMP}$$

where:

BEV = Break-Even Volume
DC = Direct Costs
GMP = Gross Margin Percentage

Let's say a salesperson has gross sales of $100,000 in a year and the product sold cost $80,000. Subtracting the latter from the former gives the gross profit: $20,000. This will also be expressed as a percentage of the gross sales:

$$GMP = \frac{\$\ 20,000}{\$100,000} = .2\ (20\%).$$

From this, the break-even volume can be calculated:

$$BEV = \frac{DC}{GMP} = \frac{\$55,000}{.20} = \$275,000.$$

This figure tells what your sales volume must be for the year in order to cover your direct costs and break even. Naturally you will aim to have gross sales far above your break-even volume so that you can contribute to the profits of your company (and be indispensable as a salesperson).

Knowing what your volume has to be for the year doesn't give you a feeling for how you're doing on a per-call-hour basis. This can be worked out by the following formula:

$$BEV/\text{call hour} = \frac{CPCH}{GMP}$$

As in the examples above, if your sales call time is worth $68.75 per hour and your gross margin percentage is 20 percent, you can calculate your break-even volume per call hour:

$$BEV/\text{call hour} = \frac{\$68.75}{.20} = \$343.75.$$

This tells you that for every hour of sales calls (based on 800 call hours per year), you need to make $343.75 in sales to break even.

If you feel more comfortable working with calls instead of hours, simply replace hours with calls in the formulas.

The value of your time is critical when you realize that you are investing your time and you must generate an acceptable rate of return on that time. The concept of opportunity costs is pertinent. If you overinvest in an account, you have paid an opportunity cost. You don't have that wasted selling time to spend on a potentially more profitable account. If you under-invest and don't obtain as much of the account's business, you have once again paid a cost. How much time should you invest in any one account? The answer is, "It depends." While that may seem to be a nonanswer, in fact, many factors must go into the correct answer. Ultimately the concept of return on time invested (ROTI) will give you a basis for judging this key issue. Sales response analysis is your next step in this process.

Sales Response Analysis
A relationship between sales volume and the level of calling effort is depicted in Figure 7-5. Several points can be illustrated by this function. First, you typically have to "grow" the account over time. As a matter of fact, there may be a good number of calls invested before any sales are forthcoming. That is why account analysis is so important. How often did you "fall into" all of an account's business after one or two calls? These windfalls are the stuff legends are made of.

Second, if you continue to make calls and do not see growth, be careful that you are not simply thinking wishfully. If you are there, you cannot be someplace else making productive sales calls. If you cannot see or reasonably anticipate a growth in sales volume, perhaps it would be best to reevaluate the account.

Third, there is a limit. An account cannot buy any more than it can buy. As you approach saturation in terms of the

Figure 7-5

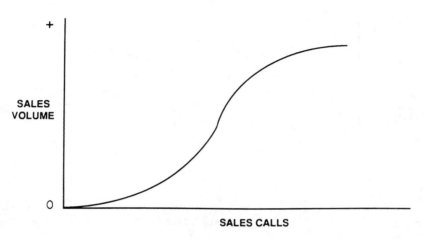

account's potential, each additional sales call generates less and less volume. This phenomenon is known as a diminishing marginal rate of return. Sales volume increases at a faster rate in the early range of the sales response function and at a slower rate as you approach the account's potential.

What, then, is the ideal number of calls to invest in an account? Ideally the point marked on Figure 7-6 is the best allocation of sales calls to the accounts.

Although you still have additional sales to capture, the cost of obtaining them is too much. Your ROTI needs to be computed. ROTI is basically a ratio of the results of your efforts to the amount of effort you put in.

$$ROTI = \frac{\text{Sales results}}{\text{Sales efforts}}$$

As with valuing your time, there are several ways of measuring sales results and effort. Sales results can be measured in gross margin, gross sales, or number of units sold. The best

Figure 7-6

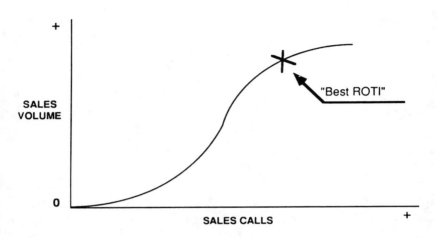

method is to use gross margin. Sales effort can be measured in the number of calls, amount of time spent on the account, or the direct cost of your time. Since we've been working with direct cost, we will continue to do so. The formula looks like this:

$$ROTI = \frac{GM}{CTI}$$

where:

$ROTI$ = Return on Time Invested
GM = Gross Margin
CTI = Cost of Time Invested

Let's say you have an account that you sold $100,000 worth of product to last year. Your gross margin percentage on the account was 20 percent. Therefore, you generated $100,000 × .20 = $20,000 of gross margin dollars. Not bad!

A question still remains: Was the account worth your time? If your cost per call hour was $68.75 as in our previous calculation and each of your forty sales calls to this account lasts about 1 hour, you can calculate the cost of time invested on this account.

$$CTI = \text{number of hours} \times CPCH$$
$$= 40 \times \$68.75$$
$$= \$2,750$$

Your ROTI on this account would have been:

$$ROTI = \frac{GM}{CTI} = \frac{\$20,000}{\$2,750} = 7.3.$$

Is this a good return? Well, it is better than 5 and worse than 10. This is a comparative number and meaningful only when it is compared to another account or to an ideal rate of return. A ROTI above 1 means you are profitable and below 1 unprofitable. If you know the ROTI for all your accounts, you have a means of allocating your time to optimize your total ROTI. If one of your accounts has a ROTI of 4 and another a ROTI of 2, you should allocate twice as much time to the 4 as the 2.

Use Worksheet 7-9 to calculate the ROTI on your accounts. If you do this on all your accounts, you will find that the ROTI varies quite a bit. The major reason is that most sellers give too much sales time to their smaller accounts. Figure 7-7 illustrates the problem with hypothetical numbers if you called on all your accounts with equal frequency.

You should be able to obtain about the same ROTI on all of your accounts regardless of their category. You can control the amount of time and to some degree the gross margin on your accounts. You can increase the ROTI on any account by increasing sales volume, improving gross margin, or reducing the cost of time invested (CTI). Sales volume can be increased subject to the account's potential, your position, and the degree of competition. Gross margin can be im-

Worksheet 7-9

CALCULATION OF ROTI

(1) Account	(2) Expected Value	(3) Gross Margin %	(4) Gross Margin $ (2) x (3)	(5) Number of Calls	(6) Cost per Call	(7) CTI (5) x (6)	(8) ROTI (4) – (7)
1.							
2.							
3.							
4.							
5.							
6.							
7.							
8.							
9.							
10.							
11.							
12.							

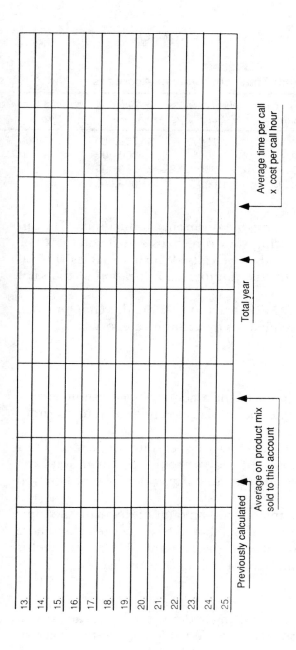

Previously calculated

Average on product mix
sold to this account

Total year

Average time per call
x cost per call hour

13.
14.
15.
16.
17.
18.
19.
20.
21.
22.
23.
24.
25.

143

Figure 7-7.
Too Much Time with Smaller Accounts

Account Category	Number of Accounts	Number of Calls	Sales Volume	Sales Volume per call
A	30	150	$ 750,000	$5,000
B	40	200	200,000	1,000
C	130	650	150,000	231
Total	200	1,000	$1,000,000	

proved by better pricing or a different product mix. CTI can be reduced by reducing your direct costs (difficult to do) or by reducing the number of calls. Which variables do you control? That's right; the number and duration of the sales calls are the keys!

You will use the ROTI calculation later in this chapter when you set your call frequencies by account category.

Workload

Workload is an estimate of the amount of your selling efforts required to penetrate the market potential of your territory effectively.

First, do you know how you are spending your time? When was the last time you kept a log of your sales time? You can't prioritize and allocate your time if you don't know how you are spending it.

Chapter 12 goes into a good amount of detail on the topic of time management. All you should be concerned about here is the relationship between the amount of time you feel is required and the amount of selling time available.

Total Accounts
How many accounts—existing and potential—by category A, B, and C are in your territory? What is your best estimate of the annual call frequency for each category?

Use Worksheet 7-10 to answer these questions. Compare your total calls required to the calls that you have available. If you're like most other salespeople, you will have to adjust your budgeted calls. Some of your possible adjustments include:

- Reduce number of planned calls, especially to B and C accounts.
- Reduce number of customers to call on.
- Reduce travel and waiting time.
- Reduce time per call.
- Reduce nonselling time.
- Use alternatives to personal calls (e.g., telephone).
- Use other forms of selling (e.g., telemarketing, inside salespeople).

Call Frequencies

Up to now you have used your experience and judgment to determine the number of calls to make on any category of account or on any one individual account. You should have been questioning these frequencies in the light of our previous discussion on ROTI. Since your time allocation has an impact on the ROTI, you should be able to use this calculation to determine the "best" call frequency.

Using your ROTI formula, which was:

$$ROTI = \frac{GM}{CTI}$$

where:

$$CTI = \text{number of calls} \times \text{cost per call,}$$

simply reformulate the calculation to solve for number of calls:

$$\text{Number of calls} = \frac{GM}{(ROTI)\,(cost\ per\ call)}.$$

In this case, you can calculate the gross margin for any one account or for a sample of accounts from a category. You know your cost per call, and you also have your target ROTI.

Worksheet 7-10

WORKLOAD ANALYSIS

Account Category	(1) Number of Accounts	(2) Estimated Calls / Year per Account	(3) Total Annual Calls (1) x (2)
A	_____ (15%)	_____	_____
B	_____ (20%)	_____	_____
C	_____ (65%)	_____	_____
TOTAL	[_____] (100%)	////////////	[_____]

     ↑   ↑

Place Total Number Here   Total Calls Required

CALLS AVAILABLE

Total Calls Available = # of Selling Days Annually x Average # of Calls per Day

Total Calls Available = _____ x _____

Total Calls Available = [_____]

For example, let's take an account with the following:

$$
\begin{aligned}
\text{Gross sales} &= \$50,000 \\
\text{Gross margin} &= 20\% \\
\text{Cost per call} &= \$50 \\
\text{Target ROTI} &= 10
\end{aligned}
$$

Therefore:

$$
\begin{aligned}
\text{Number of calls} &= \frac{\$50,000 \times .20}{(10)\,(\$50)} \\
&= \frac{\$10,000}{\$500} \\
&= 20
\end{aligned}
$$

Use Worksheet 7-11 to run this calculation on a sample of five accounts in each category. This procedure will give you a good estimate of your call frequency by category of account. You may come to find that this number is consistent with the call frequency that you have been using for your A, B, and C accounts, or you may be quite surprised.

The territory strategy portion of your territory plan primarily addresses the deployment issue, putting your resources where they will pay off the most. You must also develop an account-by-account strategy in terms of how you are going to work individual accounts from a qualitative perspective. We will discuss these issues in Chapter 8.

At this stage, the analysis phase of your territory strategy is completed. You have collected a lot of data on individual accounts. It makes sense to consolidate this information into your book of business—the account profiles.

Account Profiles

Worksheet 7-12 provides a good format for organizing your information. Modify the worksheet to fit your unique requirements. A brief explanation of each section follows:

I. Contains the account's demographics.
II. Identifies by title and role the people involved in the purchase decision.
III. Attempts to understand the account's business. What are they selling to whom and at what volumes?
IV. Addresses questions about buying practices. When do they buy? How often do they buy? What quantities are purchased? How do they buy?

Worksheet 7-11

CALL FREQUENCY ANALYSIS

Category		Account (1)	Gross Sales (2)	Gross Margin % (3)	Gross Margin $ (4) (2) (3)	Cost per Call (5)	Target ROTI (6)	Number of Calls (4) ÷ (5) (6)
A	1							
	2							
	3							
	4							
	5							
B	1							
	2							
	3							
	4							
	5							
C	1							
	2							
	3							
	4							
	5							

    V. Summarizes the amount and type of products purchased and your share of this business.

   VI. Evaluates the direction and values of the account.

  VII. Identifies the purchase criteria used by this account to evaluate products and vendors.

VIII. Details the primary competitors for this account, including their respective shares, strengths, and weaknesses.

   IX. Summarizes your company/product strengths and weaknesses on this account.

    X. Summarizes the problems and opportunities on this account.

   XI. Defines and dates your objectives on this account (e.g., sales objectives or call objectives dealing with obtaining a selling position within the account).

Worksheet 7-12 should be completed for all of your accounts and targeted prospects. You will add more information to your key accounts profile in Chapter 8.

Territory Tactics

How will you allocate your call time to your portfolio of accounts in various geographic areas of your territory? Selling time, travel time, and waiting time are at issue. Figure 7-8 describes the elements.

Call Schedules

A call schedule addresses the issue of programming your sales calls to various categories of accounts over a period of time. The call frequency that you developed earlier in this

Worksheet 7-12 (part 1)

ACCOUNT PROFILES

I

Account Name _____ Account Classification [ ]

Primary Location: Address _____

City _____ State _____ Zip _____

Primary Location: Address _____

City _____ State _____ Zip _____

Telephone _____/_____/_____ Fax _____/_____/_____

Type of Business _____

Segment Label _____

Primary S.I.C. _____

II   BUYING CENTER

Name	Title	Role				
		User	Influencer	Buyer	Decider	Gate keeper

Worksheet 7-12 (part 2)

ACCOUNT PROFILES

III. ACCOUNT PRODUCT ANALYSIS   (What does account sell, to whom?)

Major Products   Major Markets   Approximate Sales

_____   _____   _____

_____   _____   _____

_____   _____   _____

_____   _____   _____

_____   _____   _____

_____   _____   _____

_____   _____   _____

                                          TOTAL SALES   _____

IV. BUYING PRACTICES   (List any unique factors that influence the way this account purchases.)

_____

_____

_____

_____

_____

_____

V. ACCOUNT POTENTIALS   (What does this account buy?)

Product Name   Sales Potential   Our Sales   Share of Account

_____   _____   _____   _____

_____   _____   _____   _____

_____   _____   _____   _____

_____   _____   _____   _____

_____   _____   _____   _____

_____   _____   _____   _____

Worksheet 7-12 (part 3)

ACCOUNT PROFILES

VI. ACCOUNT'S PRIORITIES AND GOALS

Long Term   Short Term

_____   _____
_____   _____
_____   _____
_____   _____
_____   _____
_____   _____
_____   _____

VII. ACCOUNT'S NEEDS   IMPORTANCE

High   Average   Low

_____   ☐   ☐   ☐
_____   ☐   ☐   ☐
_____   ☐   ☐   ☐
_____   ☐   ☐   ☐
_____   ☐   ☐   ☐
_____   ☐   ☐   ☐

VIII. COMPETITION

Name	% Share of Account	Strengths	Weaknesses
_____	___	_____	_____
		_____	_____
		_____	_____
		_____	_____
_____	___	_____	_____
		_____	_____
		_____	_____
		_____	_____
_____	___	_____	_____
		_____	_____
		_____	_____

ACCOUNT PROFILES

IX. ACCOUNT'S PRIORITIES AND GOALS

Your Company / Product Strength _____

_____

_____

_____

_____

Your Company / Product Weaknesses _____

_____

_____

_____

_____

X. PROBLEMS / OPPORTUNITIES

_____

_____

_____

_____

_____

_____

XI. ACCOUNT OBJECTIVES

Objective   Target Date

_____   _____

_____   _____

_____   _____

_____   _____

_____   _____

_____   _____

Figure 7-8

TERRITORY TACTICS

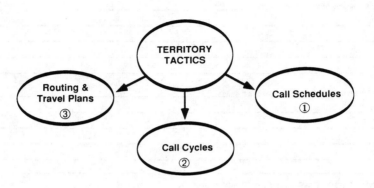

chapter reflects the best ROTI on the various categories of accounts. The question is, How do you make sales calls to these various categories of accounts in your territory over a week, month, or year? Call schedules typically tell you when to call on a specific account and who to talk to over a week. The call frequencies tell you how often to call. Your call schedule is a "to-do" list filled out in advance.

Worksheet 7-13 is a call schedule. Fill out this form the week before you actually make the calls. This form forces you to set priorities and keep on track. Obviously the schedule may be interrupted, but you at least have a benchmark to get back to.

Call Cycles

Call cycles represent the period of time it takes you to work your territory consistent with your call frequencies and the number of accounts in your territory. For example, a call cycle of two weeks means that you see all of your A accounts in two weeks, about half of your B's, and about a quarter of your C

WEEKLY CALL SCHEDULE

Salesperson:			Calls Planned — Week of:				
	CALLS TO BE MADE			**CALLS MADE**			
Date	Company	Contact(s)	Objective	Results	Action To Be Taken	Date of Next Call

155

accounts. Your call frequency on the A accounts dictates your call cycle. For example:

Category	Accounts	Week Number			
		1	2	3	4
A	Hamway	X	X	X	X
	Able	X	X	X	X
	Smith	X	X	X	X
B	Williams	X		X	
	Abbot	X		X	
	Frank		X		X
	Lewis		X		X
C	Richards	X			
	Field		X		
	Jones	X			
	Koch		X		
	Hoffman			X	
	Johnson			X	

It is important that you sequence your calls based on ideal call frequencies, but do not get too involved with the mathematics of this question. There are several factors that may mitigate this process for your type of selling. You may not have a set number of calls available in any call cycle, a fixed interval between calls may not be realistic, or your accounts may not be distributed equally geographically. Generally, unless you are a route salesperson, do not be overly concerned with call cycles.

Some rules of thumb that may help you in this regard are presented in Figure 7-9 but remember, your territory and your accounts are unique.

Routing and Travel Plans

Everyone has heard of the traveling salesperson problem. How can you route a salesperson through his or her territory while maximizing customer contact and minimizing travel

Figure 7-9

CALL CYCLES

Account Category	Suggested % of Your Sales Calls
A	35%
B	25%
C	40%

No. of Customers	500 Calls per Year	1,000 Calls per Year	2,000 Calls per Year
50	A every 2 weeks B every month C every 2 months	A every week B every two weeks C every month	A twice a week B once a week C every 2 weeks
100	A every month B every 2 weeks C every 4 months	A every 2 weeks B every month C every 2 months	A every week B every 2 weeks C every month
150	A every 6 weeks B every 12 weeks C every 24 weeks	A every 3 weeks B every 6 weeks C every 3 months	A every 1-1/2 weeks B every 3 weeks C every 6 weeks
200	A every 2 months B every 4 months C every 8 months	A every month B every 2 months C every 4 months	A every 2 weeks B every month C every 2 months
250	A every 10 weeks B every 20 weeks C every 40 weeks	A every 5 weeks B every 10 weeks C every 20 weeks	A every 2-1/2 weeks B every 5 weeks C every 10 weeks

time? Statisticians and operations researchers have applied a lot of effort and mathematical programming to this question.

You should strive to be cost effective while generating market impact in your territory. There is some science involved, but a good portion of it is an art form. A simple logic for developing your routing plan is to start identifying all of your accounts on a map of your territory. Use different colored pins to indicate A, B, and C accounts. Using your A accounts and their call frequency, divide your territory into some logical subsets. Each subset should contain all three categories of accounts if possible. Then work all of your A accounts in a subset and an appropriate number of B and C accounts.

Then move to the next subset and do the same thing. The key is not to work the A's, B's, and C's at the same call frequency. "Just happened to be in the neighborhood" calls on a C account every time you are calling on a nearby A account must be guarded against.

Territory Control

Evaluating your sales performance is a major tool for improving sales and lowering marketing costs. The collection and analysis of sales activity data will tell you what you are doing as well as why. This is the only way of discovering your strengths and weaknesses, as well as what to do about them. You can stand back and see your effectiveness objectively in the same way a manager would.

There are four phases to the control of a sales territory: standards of performance, collection of data on actual performance, performance analysis, and corrective action.

Standards of Performance

Every experiment has a baseline to which the results are compared. The standards you set up for your sales territory and individual accounts are the objectives you set up previously. These range from total sales volume for the territory to small details about one particular account. Measure your performance both quantitatively and qualitatively.

Data Collection and Record Keeping

Paperwork is an unavoidable part of our lives. In sales, it is part of an ongoing routine, which simply becomes second nature. The records you keep serve to refresh your memory, evaluate your performance, and reflect trends in account and market activities. It is important that you know which records are valuable and which are a waste of time. Develop the ability to design your own forms so that you can collect data on your personal goals and objectives. You should keep certain standard records.

Customer File

This consists of 3 × 5 cards with customer information on them: company name, address, telephone number, buying criteria, important buyers, customer's personal style, past sales, needs, competitors, and so on.

Prospect File

This contains the same kinds of available information as customer files but is kept separate until a sale is made. After the sale, the card is transferred to the customer file.

Tickler File

This file is basically a calendar. Make a new set of 3 × 5 cards based on your customer and prospect files. Arrange them by month and day to cover an entire year. The cards for the coming three months are broken down into individual days, whereas more distant months are not as detailed yet. As time goes by, upcoming months are broken down into individual days so that specific notes can be made on each day card.

The tickler file helps you plan your time and keep track of appointments. If you have to call on an account every other Thursday, write that on the appropriate card in the file. In your planning time, you can pull the cards for the coming week and see your commitments.

You may want to use different colored index cards to distinguish between customers and prospects; A, B, and C accounts; and even market segments or geographical locations. Too many colors can become confusing. Decide on the best system for you. Cross-reference the tickler file to your customer and prospect files so that you can go from one to the other quickly for pertinent information.

Sales and Customer Service Reports
This is a daily or weekly form that lists all of your calls and details about them: type of call (personal, telephone, letter), class of account, results, time required, needed follow-up, and so on. At the same time you should enter relevant data in your customer or prospect files and any new appointments in your tickler file. This master sheet lets you determine at a glance how you spent your week.

Expense Reports
Keep a record of all your expenses on a daily basis. They should be keyed to the customer or customers you spent the money on. In addition, note the classification of the account and type of expenditure. Expenses include gas, tolls, hotel, taxis, and meals.

Summary Reports
These are reports that you make out at the end of each month and at the end of each planning period. They summarize the following areas:

1. *Sales.* Volume in units and dollars; volume by customer and market segment; percentage increase or decrease over previous period; percentage of sales to calls.
2. *Account.* Number of accounts contacted; number of new accounts; percentage sold; number of accounts lost; number of new prospects.
3. *Profits.* Gross profit by market segment; overall territory profit; profit margins; ROTIs.
4. *Selling expenses.* Total expenses; expenses per call; expenses per geographic locale; expenses per account classification.
5. *Qualitative ratings.* Your strong points for the period in question; your weak points; areas of improvement; information needed for more effective sales.
6. *Miscellaneous.* Types of promotions used and their effec-

tiveness; number of telephone calls made and their outcomes; sales aids used; number of customer complaints filed; total commissions; number of days and hours worked; and so on.

As you can see, there is plenty of room for expanding the summary file to suit your needs. Often your company will give you forms that you are required to submit periodically. If these suffice for all your data, then you are in luck. If not, make up your own forms. The insights you gain will be well worth the effort required to keep these records.

Analyzing Records and Correcting Problems

Periodically sit down with your records, summarize them, and analyze what has happened while you were busy working. In this chapter we have given you the tools to determine your strengths and weaknesses from these records. You now need to determine the causes of any problems that may be evident. Analyzing your problems will allow you to deal with them before they have a negative effect on your sales or your reputation. Problems usually occur slowly, so you can intervene at an early stage only if you monitor your territory.

Ask yourself some questions to try to pinpoint areas that need work:

1. "What unnecessary activities am I undertaking?" Often salespeople will call on a C account simply because they are in the neighborhood. The fact that the time could be better spent elsewhere occurs to them only after the fact. Try to think of the activities in your day that you can cut out without missing them.

2. "What am I doing that can be done by someone else?" If you are in a position to delegate tasks, do so whenever possible. It is important to be objective in your

evaluation of whether the other person can do the job. We often operate under the assumption that only we can do a specific task when, in fact, someone else could do it. This is especially important to keep in mind when you realize how much your time is worth compared to a coworker's.

3. "What activities should I be engaged in that I'm not?" This includes things like promotional activities, public relations, personal education, prospecting, planning, and time management.

4. "Have I set the right priorities?" That is, do you spend your time where it is most cost-effective? Do you think in terms of your ROTI when planning business activities?

The Five Commandments of Territory Planning

Managing your territory can make or break you. It's as much a part of selling as the face-to-face sales process itself. So:

1. Analyze your territory, products and services, market segments, competition, accounts, and trends.
2. Set objectives based on your territory's potential rather than your historic sales.
3. Plan a strategy for the territory in general and specifically for your individual accounts.
4. Keep accurate records.
5. Analyze your records periodically and set new objectives based on this analysis.

8

Key Account Selling

KEY accounts can generate 80 percent of your success. This chapter focuses on strategies to maintain your base of business or capture new accounts. Key accounts are in the Star or Question Mark segments (Chapter 6) and are categorized as A accounts (Chapter 7). A key account is any account of strategic importance in terms of immediate business, image or stature in a segment, growth potential, potential to influence other firms, defensive posturing, or technological joint venturing.

A key account carries weight for a multitude of reasons. Selling to these accounts is critical and requires a significant amount of planning. If you develop marketing plans for *just* these key accounts, you should be a fairly successful seller.

Nature of Key Accounts

Key accounts typically involve multiple products, multiple sales contacts, multiple site locations, and multiple selling steps. They tend to be rather large organizations. Robert Nesbit, a consultant and trainer, suggests that these key accounts may be slow to change for a variety of reasons:

- The diffusion of buying authority. One person seldom has the authority to make a final decision.
- There tends to be organizational resistance to change because of the vested interests of the various functional areas.
- Many times the emotional aspects of this vested interest outweigh the rationale, logic, or inherent worth of the change.
- Typically communications in a large organization are difficult, which means that no one person ever knows everything that is going on.
- Most large organizations are geared to carry out many routines in a very predictable fashion. They are not structured to create, accept, or accommodate changes.

When you work key accounts, you function as an agent of change. This role is rather difficult and must be carefully orchestrated. Your job is to enable these firms to act in their own self-interest, notwithstanding the fact that they may not fully understand what are their "best" interests.

According to Nesbit, you should develop the following attitude to function more professionally as a key account seller:

- An ability to live with the longer time sequence associated with decision making. If you attempt to speed up the process, you usually come out on the short end.
- A willingness to work multiple contacts within the buying organization and to utilize all the resources within your firm to assist you.
- Patience and a willingness to work your account plan as opposed to reacting and making emotional decisions or sidetracking your program.
- A research mentality. The more data and information you can bring to bear, the more your status and value to the account increase.

- An ability to plan and plan—step by step, person by person, situation by situation, and product by product.
- An ability to coordinate and orchestrate the members of the buying center with those of the selling team.
- Political savvy, problem-solving expertise, and street smarts.

What, then, is a key account plan? It is simply a marketing plan developed for an individual account. Your key account plan has the same steps as the territory plan you developed in Chapter 7. Specifically, the steps are:

1. Situation analysis
2. Objective(s) setting
3. Strategy formulation
4. Program formulation (tactics)
5. Control or evaluation

The remainder of this chapter details these five steps.

Developing a Key Account Plan

Situation Analysis

This section details the critical information that you will need to understand regarding each key account. A logical starting point is the account profile (Worksheet 7-12) that you completed previously.

Two components go into your situation analysis:

1. Selling task analysis
2. Competitive analysis

Each of these components requires a significant amount of data collection and data analysis. Much of this data collection is normally obtained as part of your call-by-call selling routine. However, for key accounts you must become an active researcher. Most of the published sources that you have used previously are beneficial. You will also have to become an active interviewer in order to obtain specific data about the account to supplement the published information.

Selling Task Analysis

The purpose of your selling task analysis on each key account is to determine the type of purchase they are making, the stage in the buying process, the people in the buying center, their roles, their relative degree of influence, the criteria they will use, and their involvement in each stage of the buying process. You have already discussed some of these elements in Chapter 5 but on a segment level. You must now do the same at the key account level.

Type of purchase. Is this account faced with a new task, modified rebuy, or straight rebuy? The amount of uncertainty and risk will dictate the category. Refer to Chapter 5 for more detail on these categories.

Buying process. The buying phases discussed in chapter 5 are also relevant for key account planning. Determine where your key account is in its decision sequence:

- Anticipation or recognition of a problem (need)
- Determination of characteristics and quantity of needed item
- Description of characteristics and quantity of needed items
- Search for qualification of potential sources
- Acquisition and analysis of proposals
- Evaluation of proposals and selection of suppliers
- Selection of order routine
- Performance feedback and evaluation

Buying cycle. These are some very basic questions relating to the timing of the purchase—for example:

* When do they buy?
* How much do they buy?
* How often do they buy?

The buyers. You have to identify the players, their roles, the criteria they use, and their relative degree of influence or power in the decision. The answers may vary for different key accounts or for different types of purchases at the same account.

A good illustration of the players and their roles is presented in Figure 8-1.

The buying center roles of User, Gatekeeper, Decider, Purchaser, and Influencer provide insight and strategy for work-

Figure 8-1

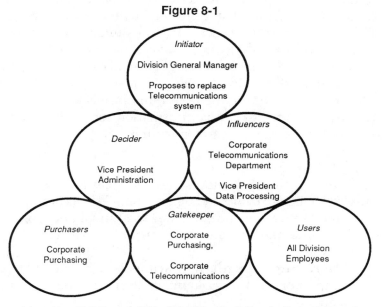

Adapted from T. V. Bonoma, "Major Sales: Who *Really* Does the Buying?" *Harvard Business Review* 61 (May–June 1982): 114.

Figure 8-2

TYPE OF POWER

Type of Power	Direction
Reward	Control of monetary, social or organizational rewards for compliance
Coercive	Control of monetary or other punishments for non-compliance
Attraction	Willingness on the part of others to comply because they like you
Expert	Others comply because of actual or perceived knowledge or technical skills
Status	Compliance given because of organizational title or position

Adapted from T. V. Bonoma, "Major Sales: Who *Really* Does the Buying?" *Harvard Business Review* 61 (May–June 1982): 114.

ing the account. What criteria does each player use to evaluate your offer? At what stage in the buying process do these criteria take on importance? Typical categories of criteria relate to products, services, economics, or relationships.

The degree of influence each of these players exerts in this decision process should also be evaluated. Figure 8-2 illustrates the sources of buying power and influence.

Figure 8-3 integrates this information for a hypothetical industrial waste-water treatment system.

Competitive Analysis
You must identify and understand the competitors you are going to challenge or defend against on a key account.

Use the same logic and tools you used in Chapter 6. The basic areas that must be addressed include:

- The relative strengths and weaknesses of you and each competitor on this account in terms of the account's needs

Figure 8-3

BUYING CENTER – WASTE-WATER TREATMENT PROJECT

Firm Acme / Jones   Type of Purchase: ☒ New Task   ☐ Modified Rebuy   ☐ Straight Rebuy

POSITION	POLE					Relative Influence	Evaluation Criteria	Stages of Involvement
	User	Influencer	Buyer	Decider	Gatekeeper			
Plant Engineer	X	X		X	X	High	Technical	1 - 3, 9
Staff Engineer		X			X	Medium	Technical	1 - 3, 9
Purchasing			X	X	X	Low	Service	5 - 8
Vice President Manufacturing	X	X		X		High	Performance Economic	6, 7
Vice President Finance		X	X			Medium	Economic	6, 8
Consulting Engineer		X			X	High	Technical	1 - 3, 9
Government Regulator		X				High	Performance	1, 2, 9

Buying Phases:
1. Problem Recognition
2. Type of Solution
3. Specifications
4. Indentify Sources
5. Acquire and Analyze
6. Evaluation of Proposals
7. Selection of Vendor
8. Purchase + Installation
9. Performance Evaluation

- The relationships and other factors that can influence decision making
- The importance of this account to you and to each competitor
- The account's perception of you and your organization
- The chances of this account's being influenced by your competitors' initiatives

Objective Setting

Each of your key accounts should have both long-term and short-term business and program objectives. What are you trying to accomplish by when? These objectives could address business goals such as sales volume, account share, product mix, or profitability. They might also address issues of a performance nature, such as sales calls, contacts made, specifications evaluated, or prototype evaluated.

The usual criteria to evaluate objectives should be used. Your objectives should be realistic, quantifiable, and for a specific period of time.

Strategy Formulation

How will you achieve your objectives on this account? In general, you must address the following questions:

1. What can you do to create the greatest overall benefits for this account?
2. What could you do to assist those responsible in accepting this offering?
3. What could you do to create a competitive differential in terms of:
   - price?
   - delivery?
   - availability?

- technical support?
- service?
- quality?
- performance?
- knowledge of account's business?
- you?

4. What resources do you require to make it all happen?
   Examples are:
   - Selling tools
   - Account information
   - Organizational support
   - Management support
   - Budget
   - Time

Program Formulation

These are the action steps that come out of your account strategy(s). They should include a consideration of:

- What is to be done
- Who is to do it
- By when
- With what effect

These steps leading up to the critical decisions should be planned in terms of:

- List of key contacts
- Contact sequence
- Description of sales approach
- Description of selling tactics
- Identification of number of calls, by whom, and objectives of each call

Control or Evaluation

Address the impact of each step in your program and relate its effects to the overall objectives you have developed for this account. Dates and measurement of impact must be in place in order to make these comparisons.

Key Questions

Figure 8-4 summarizes the critical questions that you should address in your key account plan.

Figure 8-4

KEY ACCOUNT PLANNING LEVELS

LEVEL	ILLUSTRATIVE QUESTIONS
Environmental	How will current economic projections for the industry and the economy affect the purchasing plans of this organization?
Organizational	What are the unique company attributes and procurement attributes that will influence buyer behavior?
Product-Specific	How far has the firm progressed in the buying process? What type of buying situation does this purchase represent for the organization? To what degree will organizational buyers perceive risk in purchasing this product?
Group	Will the decision be made by an individual or a group? Who are the members of the buying center? What is each member's relative influence in the decision? What is the style of each member? What is the power base of each member of the buying center?
Individual	What criteria are important to each member of the buying center in evaluating prospective suppliers? How do potential suppliers rate on these criteria?

9

Prospecting:
The Sales Pipeline

IMAGINE that you are in the plant business. You grow house
plants and carry twelve varieties. Each blooms in a different
month of the year, so you have a different plant available each
month. Each of these plants requires twelve months to grow
from seedling to full bloom. Each plant requires attention
once a month: feeding, watering, pruning, and rotating. You
therefore set up a schedule in which you plant the seeds a year
in advance and then every month do what is required to
continue or start the growth of each plant. The payoff doesn't
come until a year after you've started, but each month there-
after a new plant will be ready to sell. You're all set—unless
you forget a step one month. You will then discover your
oversight many months down the line. By then, however, it's
too late. In the plant business, you can't plant the seeds on the
thirteenth of the month and expect to have a sale on the first.

The development of your business as a salesperson also
requires investing in a future payoff. The time lag between
planting your seeds and reaping the rewards varies. Each
month, however, you must do what is necessary to ensure a

future yield. The maintenance and growth of your business requires that you:

1. Continually replenish your source of prospective clients.
2. Qualify prospects to determine their eligibility as clients.
3. Study the needs of each prospect.
4. Propose solutions to prospects' problems.

Routinely engaging in these activities will provide a smooth flow of income in the future. A failure to tackle these activities conscientiously will create a sales slump. A sales slump or flat sales are in large part attributable to negligence on the part of the salesperson. Throughout the years we have found that many salespeople focus their efforts entirely on their existing customers rather than devoting a portion of their sales time to prospecting. In order to maintain a steady flow of sales, you must maintain a pool of prospects to feed into your sales pipeline.

The illustration in Figure 9-1 demonstrates the steps necessary in creating an effective sales pipeline.

At the top of your pipeline are all the firms in your target market segments. Through the process of qualification, you reduce this group to a manageable number and select those that represent the greatest opportunity for you. Do not confuse a prospect with a lead. A lead, by definition, is a business that might become a prospect. Once a lead has been qualified, it becomes a prospect. You might consider the following list of questions when trying to determine if a lead is in fact a prospect for you:

1. Does this firm need the products or services I have to offer?
2. Does this firm perceive a need or a problem that may be satisfied by my product or service?

Figure 9-1

SALES PIPELINE

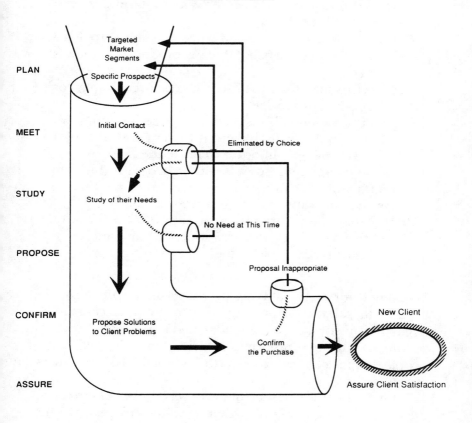

175

3. Does this firm have a sincere desire to fulfill this need or solve this problem?

4. Can this firm's desire to fulfill needs or solve problems be converted into a belief that my product or service is needed?

5. Does this firm have the financial resources to pay for my product or service?

6. Will this potential prospect's purchase be significant enough to be profitable given the amount of time I will have to invest in order to make the sale?

7. Is the competition so well entrenched with this firm that it will take an inordinate amount of my time to get the sale, thus making it unprofitable?

8. Will there be future opportunities with this firm, or will this be a short-term investment of my time?

9. Is this firm accessible to me?

Locating leads and qualifying prospects are particularly important to salespeople selling directly to final consumers (e.g., in life insurance, automobiles, and real estate). Yet prospecting is also an important activity for industrial salespeople due to the need for growth and the loss of customers over time.

To the industrial salesperson, prospecting is, in large part, the process of acquiring basic demographic knowledge. This might entail identifying all firms in the industries you target, their revenues, the products they produce, and the number of employees. This information can be obtained from a multitude of commercial sources.

Sources of Prospects

There are many methods used to generate prospects. The methods and sources used by industrial sellers versus final consumer sellers vary, yet some overlap does exist. Figure 9-2 identifies the methods that each might use.

Industrial	**Final Consumer**
Existing customers	Existing customers
Other prospects	Other prospects
Company leads	Company leads
Direct mail	Direct mail
Directories	Directories
Trade associations	Friends and social contacts
Conventions and trade shows	Professional groups
Newsletters	Centers of influence
Chamber of commerce	Canvassing
Government publications:	Tip clubs
Federal, state and local	Study groups
	Seminars and classes
	Personal observation
	Public speaking

Existing Customers

Satisfied customers represent an excellent source of prospects for both industrial and consumer salespeople. They talk with their friends, associates, and peers about their purchase and may mention your name. Occasionally a customer may volunteer the name of an associate, but this is unusual. You have to probe your customers for referrals in a professional and tactful manner. If you push too hard, your customers may become apprehensive about assisting you. Probing for referrals is a habit you might engage in after each sale or call. If you are always tactfully asking customers for referrals, perhaps they will think of some for you even when you are not there. If nothing else, they will respect your enthusiasm.

Most professional salespeople say the most effective way to obtain referrals is to ask specific leading questions. One way of doing this is to review your list of qualifying criteria for prospects. Choose one criterion and base your question on it.

If your first question doesn't produce any leads, run down your list of qualifying criteria and ask similar questions. Be sure to phrase the question so that it is open-ended rather than requiring a "yes" or "no" answer.

When a customer is giving you referrals, especially more than one, jot them down without analyzing them. After he or she has finished, you can go back and question your customer on qualifying details.

Your customers are some of the most valuable resources for referrals that you have. They know other business people in their field and are in the best position to recommend you to them. For this reason, ask your client if you can mention his or her name when contacting someone to whom he or she referred you.

Other Prospects

Prospects beget prospects. Many new salespeople assume that if a prospect doesn't buy, then there is no potential left in the relationship. Not so. A prospect can be asked for referrals in the same way that established clients are asked. With a prospect, however, it is paramount that you create a professional business relationship before asking for referrals. If you are perceived as being credible, trustworthy, and ethical, your prospect will have no qualms about referring you to others. In fact, the better your relationship is with a prospect, the harder that person will work to think of referrals for you. People are happy to help those they like.

Company Leads

Your company can furnish you with some high-quality leads. It procures leads from mailing programs, telephone solicitation, advertising, existing clients, and other sources. Sometimes your company will evaluate the quality of the lead for you.

Company leads have the advantage of giving you credibility simply by virtue of being associated with your firm. Thus, you can immediately establish a trusting relationship and work on studying the prospect's problems. The prospects who come directly to your company often do so out of need. They may be shopping around for a particular product or service. The first salesperson to get to them can often make the sale if he or she handles it right. This is also true with competitive bidding. The first person to contact the prospect has the advantage. He or she can get information to which others might not have access. Being first, he or she will find the prospect still tolerant and willing to answer a lot of questions.

Direct Mail

Direct mail as a means of prospecting offers the major advantage of allowing you to reach a large number of target segment firms without being physically present. There are two basic kinds of direct mail strategies: one-time mailings and campaigns. A one-time mailing is aimed at generating an immediate response to an attractive offer. The campaign or conditioning method seeks to make the prospect increasingly aware of you as a viable answer to needs in a particular area. This involves a long-term campaign to create confidence and interest in your abilities as a professional salesperson. Direct mailings should be followed by personal telephone calls within two to four weeks after the mailing. Although this is time-consuming, it can significantly increase your "hit" ratio.

Mailing Lists

No matter how effective your direct mail letter is, if you send it to the wrong prospects, you've wasted your time and money. Who you mail to is as important as what you mail.

Where will you get your mailing lists? In every major city there are firms that compile mailing lists that you can rent for

$25 or more per thousand names. Renting a list from a list broker offers many advantages:

1. *Categorized lists.* A list broker has already taken the time to classify lists by many different variables, such as geographic location, yearly income, demographics, age, or interests. The larger the broker is, the greater your choices will be. You may be able to save time in qualifying your prospects by asking for a specific type of list.

2. *Business expense.* Renting a mailing list is a business expense and therefore often tax deductible.

3. *Zip-code ordered.* When you're sending out a mailing to more than 200 addresses, you can take advantage of bulk mailing rates if you separate the mail into groups by zip code. A rented list is already categorized by zip code, saving you hours of work. Bulk mail permits must be obtained from the post office but are worth the nominal fee.

4. *Computer ready.* The mailing list you get from a broker is available on labels. You can then employ someone to put the labels on your mailing packages automatically.

5. *Clean and updated.* Most list brokers guarantee that the list is current and has no "dirty" addresses on it. (Dirty addresses are those that cause the letter to come back marked "addressee unknown" or "return to sender.")

Personal Mailing List

As a professional salesperson, you should develop your own file of people to whom you'll send mailings. This file can be accumulated over time and, like any other list, needs to be cleaned periodically. Whenever you meet a prospect, trade business cards. Don't immediately put that card on your mailing list. First, qualify all new prospects for your personal mailing list just as you would if you planned to call on them in person.

When compiling your mailing list, it pays to be organized. Have separate lists with categories, such as:

- Customers already doing business with the company
- High-potential prospects
- Low- to medium-potential prospects
- Centers of influence
- Friends, relatives, and others

Then determine when each of these groups should be contacted and how often. For example, you may want to contact existing customers on a quarterly basis and low-potential prospects once a year. Mark your calendar and devise other systems for organization. This work pays off in the long run.

Typically direct mail yields a low percentage return. Anything from 1 to 3 percent is often good when you figure in the cost of developing the letter, postage, mailing lists, and so on. The sales on just 1 to 3 percent can be quite sizable, however. Be sure to measure the cost by average sale expected. You want people to be reminded of you and your ability to be of service to them in some way.

Directories

Your local public library has directories on everything imaginable. Whether you're scouting out prospects in a particular area or creating a mailing list, directories will save you time and energy. Some directories specify people to contact, such as corporate officers or department heads. Polk publishes a directory that lists everyone living in every city in the United States. In some situations, this can be very useful. Let's say you're selling dish antennas for satellite TV receivers. One of the things you'll want to know is who in your area can afford one. Consult the *Polk Directory*, and look people up by street address. Beside each address is the name and occupation of each resident. You are now in a position to send an introductory letter to as many people as you wish. The directory has given you their name, address, occupation, telephone number, and zip code. What more could you ask for?

You could ask for someone else to make the initial contact to determine if prospects are even remotely interested. Many companies accomplish this by having a telemarketing team. These people call, ask certain questions, and set appointments if the prospect is interested. This saves everyone time and money.

Trade Associations

If your target market consists of a specific type of business, there is a good chance that most firms in this business belong to a trade association.

The association could provide you with information on its membership. Most trade associations publish a monthly or quarterly magazine for its membership. This could keep you up to date on trends and issues in your target market industry. The trade association might also have a mailing list of its membership for sale, helpful when you are doing direct mail prospecting.

Conventions and Trade Shows

Conventions and trade shows are to a salesperson like a candy store to a child. They are gold mines for prospecting. Attend as many trade shows and conventions as practical. Whether you are sent by your company or go on your own, you'll be going to accomplish these goals:

1. Increase your knowledge of your industry.
2. Analyze the show for possible individual or company participation in the future.
3. Determine the level and type of attendance there.

4. Impress delegates with yourself and your product or service.
5. Obtain as many prospects as possible.

Conventions are planned far in advance. Do your homework before a convention or show. Find out who is attending or being represented. See if any of your company's present clients or prospects are planning to be there. Arrange to meet with them to solidify your business relationships.

At the convention, try to meet as many people as possible. Determine why they are there and what they think of the convention and its various workshops. Discuss the latest developments in your field. Ask them about their companies, and try to uncover their needs. Also attend as many workshops and seminars as possible. Be sure to take notes and save all hand-outs, programs, brochures, and literature.

After the convention, follow up on your leads and prospects. Be sure to refresh their memories as to where and how you met. Often they will have pleasant recollections of the time you spent together at the convention.

Newsletters

The rate of technical advancement in practically every field is so great that few people can keep abreast of it. If you are selling in one of these fields and you have a thorough understanding of the changes as well as a knack for writing, you're in a prime position to produce a newsletter.

Let's use personal computers as an example. The home and small business computer market changes almost daily as new models and options are introduced. As an enterprising salesperson, you could develop a newsletter in which you call attention to new products, services, and technological improvements. Mailing a monthly newsletter of this type would be a service to your clients and prospects. They would appreciate your saving them time and would keep you in mind as someone with whom to do business.

The difficult part for you is finding the time to read, simplify, and rewrite newsworthy information. Keep in mind that a good newsletter should be:

1. *Sent out regularly.* Remember that consistency and regularity prove how serious you are.
2. *Brief.* No advertising, fish stories, or poetry for filler—just meat.
3. *Clear.* Your writing must be concise, informative, and directed to the people to whom you're sending it.
4. *Accurate.* Your credibility is at stake. Make sure your facts are accurate.
5. *Personal.* Write your newsletter as if you were the reader's personal consultant. Giving advice and your opinion is all right as long as you make it clear that it's strictly your opinion.

Chambers of Commerce

The local chamber may prove a valuable source of prospects for most any type of business in the local area. Its job is to keep up to date on local businesses and to aid in their development. For example, if your targeted market was nonprofit organizations, the local chamber would likely have a listing. The information is relatively easy to get and is usually free.

Government Publications

The U.S. government generates more information than any other single source. The information is not very detailed, but it is a first step in the process. Often it simply provides you with an understanding of the extent to which there is opportunity in a targeted industry in a given area. There are a variety of publications derived from the Census of Business, broken down into manufacturing, wholesale, retail, and service industries.

Friends and Social Contacts

Your family and friends can provide a rich source of prospects. It's not uncommon to learn that a salesperson's friends and relatives have only a vague idea of what he or she does. Now is the time to enlighten everyone as to the exact nature of your business. This should be a two-way communication. Not only will you tell them what you do, you'll also be sensitive to their needs. Whether you can sell to them is secondary. Like any other prospect, they may be able to refer you to others. It's worthwhile to qualify your friends and relatives before contacting them. It pays to do your homework.

Once you've contacted your friends and relatives, devise a method of maintaining that contact on a regular basis. Start a mailing list and send them something periodically to keep them up to date. Newsletters, brochures, direct mail correspondence, and birthday cards will serve you well.

When you approach a friend or relative, do it in a low-keyed manner. Professionalism dictates that tact and sincerity are called for here. If you get the reputation of being overly aggressive, people will avoid you. Go about it in a matter-of-fact way at first. If they're interested, then put them on the mailing list and keep them informed. You have to be able to achieve a balance between social and business interests.

Membership in Civic and Professional Organizations

Become involved with your family, friends, and different community groups. Out of all of this will naturally come new social and business relationships. But if you join a club or organization with the sole intention of milking it for its business, you'll end up miserable in the end. People can sense when they're being used.

Let's assume that you're participating in a professional organization for the same benefits as everyone else. There's certainly nothing wrong with letting people know what you do and your willingness to be of service to them. In the natural course of conversation, we're always asked, "What do you do?" The fastest way to turn people off is launch into, "I'm glad you asked. This week we're having a half-price special." It's to your advantage simply to tell them what you do and leave it at that. Later, if you see that you may be of some service to them, you can approach them and discuss it in a relaxed and helpful way. You don't have to land every prospect as he or she appears.

Once you get to know everyone in the organization (if it's small enough for you to do so), you can try to obtain a membership list or directory. You are then in a position to contact each one, again in an informative, casual way. It's not advisable to send blanket direct mailings, unless you want to be the subject of organizational gossip. If people ask for brochures or information, by all means accommodate them. The idea is to enjoy the organization and the people in it. If you also broaden your prospect reservoir, then you've really lucked out. Chances are you will. The organizations you choose to join and participate in should be loaded with prospects within your priority target markets.

Centers of Influence

A center of influence is someone in a position to steer you to prospects or prospects to you. He or she is someone important to you for one reason or another. There are centers of influence such as a banker or accounting firm in every facet of life and business. Centers of influence are also called opinion leaders. In order to ask a favor of someone who is going to influence the opinions of others, you must build rapport with the influential person. Opinion leaders as contacts are extremely valuable in any endeavor.

Canvassing

Most people think of sales in terms of a salesperson coming to the house, "getting his foot in the door," and "giving his pitch," even to deaf ears. Canvassing is the most criticized form of generating prospects.

Before you contact people or firms in your area, they should be qualified. Because they are unsolicited prospects, study their situation to determine any obvious need for your service or product. You can then approach them in an intelligent fashion. Doing your homework will make you a credible salesperson from the beginning. This opens more doors than having a strong foot. If done with sincerity, interest, and research, canvassing can expand your prospect reservoir significantly.

Tip Clubs

Many salespeople around the country have joined together to form small "tip clubs." The purpose of these groups is to make each member aware of the resources available from the other members. This type of give-and-take results in a group synergism; the branches of each person's prospecting tree are extended farther outward. Each person is able to bring to the group his or her area of expertise, centers of influence, social networks, and business contacts. With everyone bouncing ideas off one another, a kind of professional kinetic energy develops in which everyone can gain information, cross-sell, obtain referrals, and increase the drive to achieve.

Most such groups meet on a regular basis over breakfast or lunch. They often have a short program during which a member can describe his or her product or service. Most "tip clubs" follow a few helpful guidelines:

1. *Establish a set of by-laws.* These can cover everything from the cost of lunch to ethical considerations of group interactions. An example of the latter might be that you don't use a member's name as a reference without having obtained permission.

2. *All expenses should be distributed evenly.* The fact that

one member is a lawyer and another a telephone solicitor is irrelevant. The cost of meals, meeting rooms, speakers, and materials should be divided among the group equally.

3. *Shift the burden of running the group.* Periodically the group should seek new volunteers to do whatever planning and arranging is necessary for the continuance of the meetings. This should be done in smaller increments than a year so that no one is unduly taxed.

4. *Limit membership to one representative in each field.* This will ensure that a cross-section of the community's resources is present while keeping the number of members manageable. The group could strive to have an accountant, sales reps in different fields, a lawyer, a banker, a public speaker, a writer, and so on.

Study Groups

Study groups have become an effective tool for strengthening a salesperson's career. A study group is an assemblage of individuals involved in similar yet not identical activities. They form close, business-related friendships in order to help each other grow and develop as sales professionals. At each meeting, they bring one another up to date by comparing notes on recent events, types of strategies planned, obstacles encountered and overcome, and other insights. Each member tries to strengthen the other members by offering observations, assessments, feedback, and support. Study groups become very creative, supportive environments in which each person can draw on the expertise and objectivity of others. A study group should always be kept noncompetitive. If the members are going after the same prospects, it is less likely that they will be open to and supportive of one another. A study group could be viewed as a personal board of directors.

Seminars and Classes

For the professional salesperson, appearing as a lecturer or teacher is an exciting and rewarding way to gain exposure. You can offer to teach evening classes at local colleges and adult education programs. Large corporations occasionally hold seminars to improve their employees' skills. These all provide prime opportunities for you to become regarded as an expert in your field.

The most valuable time is after a class or seminar when you socialize, listen to participants' individual needs, and schedule future contacts.

Public Speaking

Civic clubs, professional organizations, corporations, associations, and church groups are constantly seeking effective speakers to address their groups. If you can develop your skills as a speaker, you'll find this avenue to be highly rewarding and fruitful as a prospect generation source.

The speech you give as a public speaker needs to be much more general than the one you give as a lecturer or teacher. Remember not to be commercial. Focus on the broad subject under your area of expertise.

There are two effective ways to gain prospects from a public speaking engagement. One is to distribute response cards on which interested prospects fill in their names and telephone numbers. The other is to hold a drawing. Bring along a gift or offer a discount on your firm's product. To enter the drawing, the participants simply drop their business card into a box from which you will pick the winner. You'll then have scores of names to qualify later as prospects. You can also offer to send a free copy of your speech to any attendees who give you their business cards. When you mail the article, you can include information about yourself, your company, and your products/services.

Personal Observation

Prospecting can take place whether you're on the job or not. This is true, however, only when it becomes second nature. Once you have conditioned yourself to recognize a prospect in any situation, you can act on the insight with a mailing, personal contact, conversation, and so on. You'll find prospects in the newspaper, on TV talk shows, at parties, waiting in line, and in the doctor's office. The key is to have the qualifications firmly planted in your mind so that those types of people will jump out at you.

By now you see that prospects are ubiquitous. Ways of contacting them are also so numerous that they can be overwhelming. It is important for you to analyze your current sales situation and determine the sources that will be most productive for you. This will help you maximize your use of time.

The Prospecting Plan

In order to realize the maximum benefit from your prospecting efforts, you must develop and execute a comprehensive prospecting plan. A plan typically has five elements:

1. Set objectives.
2. Allocate time.
3. Determine which prospecting technique works best for you.
4. Classify prospects.
5. Evaluate your results.

The objectives set for your prospecting plan should be very similar in nature to any other type of marketing objective you develop.

Too often objectives for prospecting are stated in very broad terms—for example, "I intend to add new prospects this year." This is meaningless. Success could be defined as one new prospect this year. The time frame must be more specific; there must be a well-defined beginning and end. A good prospecting objective might be, "To add X number of qualified new prospects to my prospect list between January 1, 1990, and January 1, 1991."

Once you have established your prospecting objectives, you must allocate the necessary time. Often it is difficult to allocate sufficient time due to the demands placed on you to sell and service existing accounts, do paperwork, attend training sessions, participate in trade shows, and attend sales meetings, among other things. The investment of time in prospecting requires a long-term orientation, and this is difficult when you are being evaluated on short-term results.

The maturity of the product or service offered will have some influence over the amount of time you will be willing to allocate to prospecting. The more mature the product or service is, the less time you will devote. In the introductory and growth stages of a product's life, a proportionately larger amount of your time will be devoted to prospecting due to the expanding nature of the market.

The techniques that a salesperson elects to use is really a function of the specific situation. The discussion at the beginning of this chapter should have provided insight into the technique(s) most appropriate for you. The methods you select should be the ones that will be the most productive for you. Experiment with more than one before you decide which method(s) you will implement on a regular basis.

Once you begin to identify prospects, develop a system for classifying and recording them. This will aid in the implementation of your prospecting plan. Without such a system, your prospecting effort will become haphazard and most likely fall by the wayside. There are a number of classifications you might consider for your prospects:

- Geographical
- Potential volume
- Products sought
- Type of business

By classifying your prospects, you will be able to evaluate the status of each quickly. If you classify your prospects based on the listed criteria, you will know who your prospects are in any given geographic area. You will also be aware of their industry, the types of products they seek, and the opportunity they offer. All of this information will give you the ability to plan the sales call you will make on these prospects.

Good record keeping is an essential element of any prospecting program. All information on the prospect should be easily accessible and updated regularly. A card file is a very effective tool for keeping track of prospects. Worksheet 9-1 includes the relevant information.

The last step in the prospect planning process is the evaluation of results. Determine if you have fallen short of, met, or exceeded your prospecting objectives and why. Then revise your plan to reflect what you have learned. Determine which methods to drop or modify to fit your situation. Worksheets 9-2 and 9-3 will aid in evaluating your prospecting plan. Worksheet 9-2 provides a record of the prospecting methods you have used for different firms. Worksheet 9-3 evaluates the effectiveness of the methods you have employed by comparing your expected performance to actual performance.

Through the evaluation process you will learn to develop objectives that reflect your capabilities and the opportunities in the market. The result will be a refinement of your prospecting activities so that the time you invest in prospecting will be highly profitable to you.

Worksheet 9-1

PROSPECT DATA SHEET

Name of prospect _____

Address of prospect _____

_____

Products purchased:

   Product A_____   Product B_____   Product C_____

Product volume:

   Product A $_____   Product B $_____   Product C $_____

Type of business

SIC Code

Has prospect been qualified?   Yes   No

Actions required to:

   1. Qualify the prospect:

       •

       •

       •

   2. Follow-up:

       •

       •

       •

Worksheet 9-2

PROSPECTING METHOD IDENTIFICATION

Prospecting Performance Evaluation Form						
PROSPECTS	METHODS OF PROSPECTING					
	Company Leads	Direct Mail	Industrial Directories	Trade Shows	Trade Assns.	Other
Company A						
Company B						
Company C						
Company D						
Company E						
Company F						
Company G						
Company H						
Company I						
Company J						
Company K						

Worksheet 9-3

PROSPECTING PERFORMANCE EVALUATION

Prospecting Performance Evaluation Form				
Prospecting Method	Objectives– Planned Performance	Actual Performance	Excess (shortage)	Explanation

Monitoring Your Performance

I F you look in any management textbook, you will find that there are always three major functions that managers perform:

- Planning
- Implementation
- Control

So far we have focused primarily on the planning and implementation aspects of your sales position. This chapter is a brief overview of your control responsibilities. The basic question to be addressed is, "How are you going to measure your performance?" You cannot evaluate your objectives, strategies, or tactics unless you keep track of what you are doing. Chapter 3 discussed the organizational goals and priorities expected of you. We want to be a bit more specific here in defining the exact nature of those standards of performance.

Your job is to make sure that the organization's goals and priorities are accomplished effectively. As your own sales manager, you should develop your own measures that control your effectiveness and efficiency.

The measures you use should be the same as your sales managers should be utilizing. There are three types of performance you must measure: effort, opportunities, and results.

There are many statistics that you can use to monitor these three areas, depending on the specific circumstances of your job. Figure 10-1 lists many of the statistics that we have found in use. You may have to obtain some of the data from your financial and accounting people. Some of the data will come from your own records, and you will probably have to generate some of them, such as market and account potentials.

The key to this control function is to keep track of what you need to do to make sure you are effective and efficient. Keeping track of too many variables adds to your confusion, not your knowledge. Know what is important and what is not, and don't get confused.

FIGURE 10-1.
Performance Measures

Effort Measures

Sales calls

- Number made on current customers
- Number made on potential new accounts
- Average time spent per call
- Number of sales presentations
- Selling time versus nonselling time
- Call frequency ratio per customer type
- Calls per day
- Days worked

- Calls per day ratio $= \dfrac{\text{Number of calls}}{\text{Number of days worked}}$

- Calls per account ratio $= \dfrac{\text{Number of calls}}{\text{Number of accounts}}$

- Planned call ratio $= \dfrac{\text{Number of planned calls}}{\text{Total number of calls}}$

- Orders per call (hit) ratio $= \dfrac{\text{Number of orders}}{\text{Total number of calls}}$

Sales expenses

- Average per sales call
- Expenses as a percentage of sales quota
- By customer type
- By product category
- Direct selling expense ratios
- Indirect selling expense ratios

- Sales expense ratio $= \dfrac{\text{Expenses}}{\text{Sales}}$

- Cost per call ratio $= \dfrac{\text{Total costs}}{\text{Number of calls}}$

Nonselling activities

- Letters written to prospects
- Telephone calls made to prospects
- Number of formal proposals developed
- Advertising display set-ups
- Number of meetings held with distributors/dealers
- Number of training sessions for distributor/dealer personnel
- Number of calls on distributor/dealer customers
- Number of service calls made

- Number of customer complaints received
- Number of overdue accounts collected

Opportunity Measures

- Territory potentials
- Market segment potentials
- Account potentials
- Number of accounts
- Size of territory

Result Measures

- Total dollar contribution
- Average contribution margin
- Contribution in margin dollars per call
- Current versus past sales
- Current sales per call
- Account penetration ratio $= \dfrac{\text{Accounts sold}}{\text{Total accounts available}}$

- New account conversion ratio $= \dfrac{\text{Number of new accounts}}{\text{Total number of new accounts}}$

- Lost account ratio $= \dfrac{\text{Prior accounts not sold}}{\text{Total number of accounts}}$

- Sales per account ratio $= \dfrac{\text{Sales dollar volume}}{\text{Total number of accounts}}$

- Average order size ratio $= \dfrac{\text{Sales dollar volume}}{\text{Total number of orders}}$

- Order cancellation ratio $= \dfrac{\text{Number of cancelled orders}}{\text{Total number of orders}}$

11

Time Management

TIME is nature's greatest force. Nothing can stop it; nothing can alter it. Unlike the sun, it cannot be seen. Yet of all nature's forces, time has the most profound effect on us.

Time remains constant, but our perception of it changes. When we focus on it, it slows down. When we turn our back on it, it speeds up. Sometimes we think it is something tangible. We arrange it, divide it up, give some to our friends. Sometimes we feel it is precious; at other times we waste it. We give it the power to heal when we say, "Time heals all wounds." It can also kill, as when we live stressful lives because we "never have enough time." On a day-to-day basis, nothing is defined and redefined in our minds as much as time.

We can choose to see time as a manageable commodity and live our lives according to that assumption. The first step is to take responsibility and want to control our time. This is one of the secrets of successful people. They work at shaping those things others think are uncontrollable.

Note: Many of the ideas in this chapter were stimulated by the works of Dr. John W. Lee, Hour Power, Inc., Crawfordville, Florida, and Merrill E. Douglass, Time Management Center, Grandville, Michigan.

As a professional salesperson, you'll have to manage your time effectively. Think of yourself as a business. Imagine having an employee who comes to work and doesn't get as much done as you'd like. It wouldn't be long before you started to manage this employee's time. You would also watch him carefully to make sure he continued being productive. The same applies to you. You are your greatest boss, and your most valuable asset is time. This chapter will show you how to get the most out of this elusive resource.

Efficient versus Effective

In discussing time management, some people argue that "we need to be more *efficient* with our time!" Others claim, "Let's not worry so much about efficiency. Let's be more *effective!*" (Of course, there are always the ones who yawn and say, "It's just a matter of semantics. When do we eat?")

For the purpose of this book, we will draw a distinction between the two. *Efficiency* means doing things right. *Effectiveness* means doing the right things. Working efficiently is doing things with the least amount of wasted effort. Efficiency gets you from point A to point B via a straight line. Inefficiency goes in circles and zigzags and gets fewer miles per gallon. Effectiveness means doing the things that yield results. Effectiveness takes aim at the target and hits it, even if it's beyond you. Effectiveness *works.*

Many new salespeople, when learning about time management, ask the question, "Which should I work on first: efficiency or effectiveness?" In theory and practice, the best answer is to improve effectiveness first. Effective selling will get you sales and give you time to work on efficiency. It's much better to aim your sights at the result than to worry about the process. Too often we get bogged down in the means and lose sight of the end.

Before you can improve your use of time, you need to know

where you stand now. Taking time to analyze your habits will lead the way to more effective and efficient time management in the future.

The first characteristic to learn about is your circadian rhythm. Circadian rhythm marks the high and low points of your effectiveness during the day. Everyone has a "prime time." Some of us are morning people; others are night people. Whether this is biologically determined is secondary. What is important is to note your patterns of effectiveness. Find your best time of the day. Do you sell more in the mornings or the afternoons? Are you in a fog until noon? Once you know when you're at your best, you can organize your day accordingly.

The Time Log

In order to control your time, you have to know what you're doing with it now. We would like you to do an exercise that is going to take a maximum of a half an hour a day for fifteen days. You won't have to go on a crash diet or run three miles a day, but we guarantee that by the end of the second week, you'll have grown. You'll look the same, but you'll have grown inside. How will you know which bad habits to change unless you monitor your way of doing things? It would be like going to a doctor and saying you think you need to lower your blood pressure. Would you be happy if he or she prescribed a drug without taking your blood pressure first?

So take the time every day to complete time logs shown in part 1 of Worksheet 11-1. Fill in your activities for thirty-minute intervals throughout the day. Try not to allow more than an hour to pass without recording what you've done. It's really not as much work as it seems and will be a habit in no time.

At the end of each day, answer the daily time analysis questions shown in part 2 of Worksheet 11-1. Try to be as exact as possible in ascertaining what happened that day. Also be specific in stating the ways you'll make tomorrow better.

At the end of ten days, analyze the time logs to determine the six most important activities that you engaged in during that time. List them in the space provided in part 3 of Worksheet 11-1. At the same time, determine the six least important things you did and compute the total amount of time spent on each of these activities.

After you've written out your six most and least productive activities and the time spent on each, you will be equipped to set some time management objectives. Use the skills you learned in Chapter 3 on goal setting. Write out your objectives and develop an action plan for each. Then follow through.

Eliminating Time Wasters

There isn't anyone who doesn't waste time, and anyone who says otherwise is wasting *your* time! Of course, we really can't tell you what is a waste of your time. What constitutes a waste of time is strictly an individual judgment.

Time wasters come from the people around you, as well as from within yourself. Some time wasters are unavoidable but reducible nonetheless. You need to identify the most frequent sources of time wasters in your day. Use part 1 of Worksheet 11-2 to develop a profile of your time-wasting activities. Be honest with yourself, and base your answers on an average day. After you've completed part 1, choose the three biggest time wasters and enter them in the spaces in part 2. Then think of ways in which you will overcome the time wasters.

Worksheet 11-1

Part I: TIME LOG

TIME LOG FOR _____

DATE _____ DAY_____   **ANALYSIS**

HOUR	TIME FRAME	ACTUAL TIME	DESCRIPTION OF ACTIVITIES	COMMENTS FOR BETTER TIME USE
7	0 - 30			
	30 - 60			
8	0 - 30			
	30 - 60			
9	0 - 30			
	30 - 60			
10	0 - 30			
	30 - 60			
11	0 - 30			
	30 - 60			
12	0 - 30			
	30 - 60			
1	0 - 30			
	30 - 60			
2	0 - 30			
	30 - 60			
3	0 - 30			
	30 - 60			
4	0 - 30			
	30 - 60			
5	0 - 30			
	30 - 60			
6	0 - 30			
	30 - 60			
7	0 - 30			
	30 - 60			

Part 2: Daily Time Analysis Questions

1. What went right today? Why?

2. What went wrong today? Why?

3. What time did I start on my top-priority task? Why? Could I have started earlier?

4. What patterns do I see in my time logs?

5. What part of the day was most productive? least productive?

6. What were my three biggest time wasters today?

7. What activities need more time? Which need less time?

8. Beginning tomorrow, what will I do to make better use of my time?

Part 3: Daily Time Analysis

MY SIX MOST PRODUCTIVE ACTIVITIES

Between (Dates) _____

1.   Total Time: _____

2.   Total Time: _____

3.   Total Time: _____

4.   Total Time: _____

5.   Total Time: _____

6.   Total Time: _____

MY SIX LEAST PRODUCTIVE ACTIVITIES

Between (Dates) _____

1.   Total Time: _____

2.   Total Time: _____

3.   Total Time: _____

4.   Total Time: _____

5.   Total Time: _____

6.   Total Time: _____

Worksheet 11-2
Part 1: Time Wasters

	None	Some	A Lot
1. Overpreparing for calls	____	____	____
2. Scheduling less important work before more important work	____	____	____
3. Starting a job before thinking it through	____	____	____
4. Leaving jobs before they are completed	____	____	____
5. Doing things that can be delegated to another person (across or down; not upward)	____	____	____
6. Doing things that can be delegated to modern equipment (providing such exists in your work)	____	____	____
7. Doing things that aren't actually part of your job	____	____	____
8. Keeping too many, too complicated, or overlapping records	____	____	____
9. Pursuing prospects you probably can't sell	____	____	____
10. Paying too much attention to low-yield prospects	____	____	____
11. Handling too wide a variety of duties	____	____	____
12. Failing to build barriers against interruptions	____	____	____
13. Allowing conferences and discussions to wander	____	____	____
14. Conducting unnecessary meetings, visits, and/or telephone calls	____	____	____
15. Chasing trivial data after the main facts are in	____	____	____
16. Socializing at great length between tasks	____	____	____

Part 2: Overcoming Time Wasters

1. Time waster_____

   Strategies for minimizing

2. Time waster_____

   Strategies for minimizing

3. Time waster_____

   Strategies for minimizing

Setting Priorities

When setting your priorities, there are two famous laws to remember. The first is Parkinson's law. It states that work tends to expand to fill the time allotted for its completion. Parkinson's law makes setting priorities twice as important. If you don't know your priorities, your other work will expand to fill the extra time. It will take longer for you to accomplish less.

The second law is Pareto's principle. Pareto's principle, in this situation, states that 80 percent of your results comes from 20 percent of your efforts.

You need to spend your time doing activities that pay you more than your time is worth. You need to increase the use of your time in high-priority activities that bring the greatest payoff. It doesn't make sense to wash your car during the day when your time is worth $25 per hour or more to you. Arrange your day to take advantage of your earning potential. Identify your high-priority activities and fill out Worksheet 11-3. Think about the most important things you do from three different perspectives: your sales manager's, your clients', and your own. Then choose the six priorities that stand out regardless of perspective.

Worksheet 11-3.
High-Priority Activities

DIRECTIONS: List below the six most important activities you perform on the job in the eyes of your immediate manager, your clients/customers, and yourself. Then list the overall top six activities.

In the eyes of my sales manager:

1. _____

2. _____

3. _____

4. _____

5. _____

6. _____

In the eyes of my customers and prospects:

1. _____

2. _____

3. _____

4. _____

5. _____

6. _____

In my own eyes:

1. _____

2. _____

3. _____

4. _____

5. _____

6. _____

THE OVERALL HIGH-PRIORITY ACTIVITIES:

1. _____

2. _____

3. _____

4. _____

5. _____

6. _____

Using a "To-Do" List

A "to-do" list for each day and week is a valuable aid to managing your time. It organizes your thinking and planning onto one form in the least amount of time with the maximum amount of efficiency. Such a list is especially helpful if it coincides with the record keeping you already do for your company. After a short time, you will find yourself handling a greater volume of work without increasing your stress. You'll simply have become more efficient.

Because we are creatures of habit, it's a good idea for you to fill out your to-do list at the same time every day. This way you'll be committed to a routine and will avoid procrastination. Whether you fill it out in the evening or first thing in the morning is unimportant. Keep in mind, however, that you are often in a hurry in the morning and may be tempted to skip it. As we mentioned before, Parkinson's law states that work expands to fill the time allotted for it. Your to-do list should therefore specify the amount of time for each activity. This will keep work from expanding.

Your activities should be listed in order of priority. Work on high priorities first, and keep in mind what your time is worth. In listing the activities, it is helpful to spell out the results as well as the process. For example, you might list, "Between 12:00 and 1:00 P.M., go to manufacturer's rep luncheon and get at least three business cards from prospects." Stating when, where, and what you're going to do increases your chances of doing it successfully.

As the day goes by, check off completed activities and make any notes that seem relevant. In the evening, make out a new "to-do" list for the next day and include any activities you couldn't complete the day before. Always save your to-do lists for future reference. Worksheet 11-4 can serve as a guide.

Keeping Records of Time Use

Some companies require their salespeople to keep accurate records; others do not. The experts in time management all agree that the more records you keep, the more you will be aware of the opportunities for sales, prospecting, and improving your use of time. Examples of valuable records to keep include:

- Number of sales calls
- Number of calls resulting in interviews
- Number of interviews resulting in attempts to confirm the sale
- Number of actual sales
- Number of sales that stay on the books

Through systematic record keeping you will learn, among other things, what phase of the sale you're having trouble with. You can chart your performance to get a graphic illustration of your strengths and weaknesses.

Another highly valuable record is your daily time log. Not only will this depict your efficiency on a day-to-day basis, it will also speed your writing of monthly reports. In fact, you might be able to staple your daily time logs together to compose your monthly report. If you get in the habit of taking five minutes each day to answer the time analysis questions, you will quickly gain invaluable insight into your patterns of both productive activity and time wasting. Like written goals, daily written proof of your inefficiency will have more of an effect on your motivation than just thinking about it.

McGraw-Hill has researched for years the way salespeople use their time. Here are their statistics:

Face-to-face selling	25%
Travel and waiting	25
Administration	22
Telephone selling	17
Service	8
Eating	3

Procrastination

Procrastination is like a virus. It creeps up on you slowly, drains you of energy, and is difficult to get rid of if your resistance is low. Procrastination is a close relative of incompetence and a first cousin to inefficiency, which is why their marriage is taboo. We all procrastinate from time to time. What's important is not to do it on matters that count. You can overcome procrastination if you recognize it and take responsibility for it. Don't make yourself the victim by claiming to be lazy. Laziness means simply not caring enough to act. These suggestions will help you conquer the virus:

1. *Choose one area* in which procrastination plagues you and conquer it. Set up a procrastination priority and action steps. For example, if you're putting off calling qualified prospects, set a goal of calling on a specified number every day or week.

2. *Give yourself deadlines.* In moderation, pressure motivates. Extreme pressure debilitates. Set appointments, make commitments, and write out your goals.

3. *Don't duck the difficult problems.* Every day we are faced with both difficult and easy tasks. Tackle the difficult ones first so that you can look forward to the easy ones. If you work on the easy ones first, you might expand the time that they take in order to avoid the difficult ones waiting for you.

Many people put off difficult or large tasks because

Worksheet 11-4

TO DO LIST

Item	Priority	Time Needed	✔ Done		Scheduled Events
				8:00	
				:15	
				:30	
				:45	
				9:00	
				:15	
				:30	
				:45	
				10:00	
				:15	
				:30	
				:45	
				11:00	
				:15	
				:30	
				:45	
				12:00	
				:15	
				:30	
				:45	
				1:00	
				:15	
				:30	
				:45	
				2:00	
				:15	
				:30	
				:45	
				3:00	
				:15	
				:30	
				:45	
				4:00	
				:15	
				:30	
				:45	
				5:00	
				:15	
				:30	
				:45	
				6:00	
				Evening	

Reprinted with permission from Merrill E. Douglass, Time Management Center, Grandville, Michigan.

they appear too huge to tackle in a reasonable time frame. They feel that if they start and complete the large task at one sitting, it will prevent them from accomplishing any of the other tasks they have to do that day. The answer to this problem is to break all large or difficult tasks into their smaller subparts. Then you can do each of the subparts of the larger project over a series of days, if appropriate.

4. *Don't let perfectionism paralyze you.* This is a problem many writers have. They sit at their typewriters waiting for the "right" words to come out. What they are doing is avoiding the process of writing. You can always go back and polish those things you're unhappy with. Better yet, you can delegate the polishing to someone else.

Because humans are so susceptible to procrastination, you must work at building up your immunity to it. Effective action is the best medicine.

Handling Paperwork

The first step in handling paperwork is to do yourself the favor of reducing it. Delegate as much as you can to your secretary or other coworker. After you've reduced the quantity, you can handle the rest efficiently.

Have your secretary screen your mail and put in order of priority so that you can act on the most important pieces first. Junk mail goes at the bottom. Important mail and information go in the middle, and letters requiring an immediate response go on top. Set a time for opening your mail, and keep it the same every day. This obviously should be scheduled during an otherwise nonproductive time.

Try to answer any correspondence immediately. After you've read the letter, write your reply on the back, and give it to your secretary to type. A more efficient method is to use a dictation machine or tape recorder. Record your correspondence, and leave the rest to your secretary.

Some companies prefer to use form letters instead of replying personally. This is acceptable in some circumstances but not when you're communicating with prospects or clients.

The other mail you receive should be dealt with in the same way. Act immediately on whatever you can. If you receive a magazine, peruse it and clip out articles you intend to read. Try categorizing your reading material into three groups: articles you must read soon, articles you should read, and articles that would be nice to read. Stacking ten articles in one category is much more practical than stacking ten magazines. The magazines look like more work and discourage you from diving into them.

Naturally there will be more than mail accumulating on your desk. Adopt a policy of picking up paperwork only once. You should not look at something and put it back down where you found it. It's much wiser to take some form of activity on the item. Decide what to do with it and move it along.

One novel approach to correspondence was adopted by entrepreneur Meshulan Riklis. He simply let all but the most urgent mail ripen in his "in" box for at least three months. When it was ripe, he found that 80 percent of it didn't need to be answered.

Your Use of Downtime

Downtime normally refers to time when a machine is out of service. Your downtime includes unstructured minutes and hours during the day when you can't get anything significant accomplished: during traffic jams, in waiting rooms, when people fail to show up for appointments, and so on. You can fill this time instead of "wasting" it.

There are ways of doing nothing creatively. You can sit and

relax or meditate. You can look at your "to-do" list and change it if necessary. You can think about your goals or the obstacles that you face and how you're going to overcome them. Imagine yourself calling on an account that you've been dreading. Imagine yourself as successful, and you improve your chances of becoming successful.

Remember those articles you clipped and saved? If you carry them with you, you can read them while you're waiting. It's amazing how many little tasks can be done in ten-minute time slots. Downtime is also useful for making telephone calls. You can call ahead to your next appointment, call the office, and so on. With this in mind, you might want to write telephone numbers on your "to-do" list so they'll be readily accessible.

The important thing about downtime is to avoid wasting it. Don't fight yourself and the world. Relax and see downtime for what it is: more of that valuable asset you so desperately need—time.

Interruptions

Most people who telephone or visit you at home or work do so under a false yet unquestioned assumption that you are free and "receiving" company. No one ever calls and says, "Hi. Are you busy?" Or if they do it's, "Hi. Are you busy?" (Yes) . . . "Oh, good. . . . I wanted to tell you about this delicious pastrami sandwich I just had. . . ." Just what you need to hear in the middle of a busy day! It's no wonder so many business people have high blood pressure.

Despite the selfishness of intruders, we too operate on a false assumption. Ours is that despite their selfishness, we cannot be blunt and sound inhospitable or ungracious. We usually just grit our teeth and resent them later—not a healthy situation.

There is a place for courtesy, but courtesy does not have to extend carte blanche to callers who interrupt the flow of thoughts, destroy concentration, or impede the continuity of effort. As a professional salesperson with limited time and unlimited work, you need to cultivate a direct, diplomatic way of handling interruptions.

The Telephone Interruption

There are two ways to control the intrusion of telephone calls: a skilled secretary or an answering machine. An answering machine simply postpones the call and puts it in your hands to be returned. (Making outgoing calls will be covered in a moment.) Having a skilled secretary is more efficient and should be used if possible. You will have to communicate effectively with your secretary to determine the procedures for the four different kinds of calls you'll receive.

1. *Directing traffic:* Your secretary's first duty is to determine the urgency of the call and to whom it can be transferred. Many calls can be answered by others or by your secretary.
2. *Automatic call-back:* Some calls only you can handle but are not sufficiently urgent to warrant an interruption. Your secretary can ask the caller, "May she call you back when she is free?" or better yet, "Can you call again later?" The automatic call-back is a highly effective way to avoid intrusions.
3. *Brief interruption:* Sometimes your secretary can be helpful to you and your caller. By putting the caller on hold and asking you for a brief response to a quick question, you are saved the trouble of calling back later and the caller is satisfied.
4. *Urgent, interrupt immediately!* There will always be calls that you will predesignate as warranting an interruption. These you can handle on the spot. Few of your daily calls should fall into this category.

The Call-Back System

Even if your secretary has headed off the onslaught of calls, you have the burden of returning some of them. Unlike correspondence, calls should not be left to ripen. Create a system for returning calls that includes time-saving habits.

Determine the time of the day to return calls. You may want to choose the late morning or late afternoon. At these times, chances are greater that you'll catch the other party facing lunch engagements or leaving for the day. These time pressures will make him or her less likely to socialize on the telephone.

Information can be prepared in advance when you use the call-back system. Your secretary can pull files and gather documents you'll need to answer the client's questions— obviously a time saver for you.

Outgoing Calls

The telephone is one of life's greatest time savers. It saves time over writing letters, making trips, and meeting with people. But it can also be a great time waster. To avoid spending more time than necessary in calling people back, follow these suggestions:

1. *Curtail the length of your calls.* One effective way is to choose your opening. Don't say, "Hi, Jane; how are you?" You may be opening a can of worms. You're better off saying, "Hi, Jane. I need to ask you a few questions if you have a minute." Then launch into the questions as soon as you get the OK. It's also important to be able to terminate your calls promptly. Be decisive and say, "I guess that covers it, Jane. Thanks for your time. Speak to you soon. Good-bye." If you carry on business conversations

succinctly, perhaps people will realize you are a busy person and will not waste your time when they call you.

2. *Be organized.* List the questions or topics you wish to discuss, and have them in front of you. There's nothing worse than saying, "Uh, I forgot the other question I was going to ask you . . ." if you lose your train of thought.

3. *Group your calls by type.* If you are making sales calls, make them all at once. You'll be in a certain thinking mode and won't have to change gears for every other call.

Visitors

Visitors have the same effect as telephone calls. Again, the ideal situation is to have a secretary run interference for you in a professional, diplomatic way.

1. Authorize your secretary to handle appointments and screen visitors. If in doubt, your secretary can set up tentative appointments subject to your approval.

2. Set fixed "visiting" hours. You can't be receptive to visitors all day. Have your secretary tell people who drop by that you are busy.

3. During appointments, have your secretary monitor the visit. If it goes on for longer than normal, she or he can call or come in to tell you about an obligation you must attend to. You then have an easy way to terminate the meeting if necessary.

4. Block interruptions when you have visitors. You can't talk to someone in your office and receive telephone calls simultaneously.

5. Try not to socialize during business visits. Impress your visitor with how busy you are and hope he or she gets the hint.

6. Terminate your visits by standing up, an obvious sign that it's time to go. Walk your visitor to the door and say good-bye without standing by the door or elevator chatting.

Relaxation and Stress Reduction

In our goal-oriented, hypermotivated, money-making work-day we often deny ourselves much-needed periods of relax-ation. Like a high-powered sports car, we can be very impressive at high speeds but sacrifice distance, efficiency, and physical integrity in the process. Our bodies and minds are designed to work well if they are not overtaxed. Frequent periods of relaxation and stress reduction are important to our bodies and minds.

All too often the coffee break is abused rather than maxi-mized. People become focused on the process rather than the desired result of the break. A coffee or lunch break should be used as a time to relax so that you are more effective when you return to work. The relaxation you seek during a break should achieve three things:

1. It should provide distraction. You should get your mind off the job and preferably into the wild blue yonder. You'll feel much more refreshed when you land again.
2. It should alleviate tension. Our jobs often produce stiff-ness in the lower back, neck, and abdomen. Physical activity or relaxation exercises can relieve these tensions. Many people have changed their habits in recent years. They are no longer rushing through a big meal at the lunch counter or restaurant. Instead many people go for a run, swim, walk, or simply relax in their offices.
3. It should be short enough not to interfere severely with your workday but long enough to provide you with some benefits.

There is no denying the importance of relaxation, despite its being "unproductive." As John Wanamaker once said, "Those who do not take time for relaxation are obliged sooner or later to find time for illness."

Change Your Bad Habits

"Habit, my friend, is practice long pursued, that at the last becomes the man himself" (Evenus, fifth century B.C.).

Managing your time efficiently and effectively will require some changes in your behavior and thinking. These changes require practice. Giant strides, when looked at closely, are made up of many small steps. In "overhauling" your management of time, you too need to take small steps. We would like you to choose one area that you would like to improve. It could be procrastination, delegation, or relaxation. It's your choice—but select one area now. Take the time to fill out the Time Management Key Idea Action Plan (Worksheet 11-5). Answer all the questions thoroughly so that you can devise a solid goal and some action steps. Start today doing those things that will make you a better manager of your time. After you've improved in one area, choose another and use the key idea action plan to define the steps. In this way, you will practice the activities that will later become your good habits.

Worksheet 11-5.
Time Management Key Idea Action Plan

What is the idea I would like to implement?

What are the potential obstacles?

Why do I want to implement this idea? What's in it for me?

What is my action plan? How will I specifically implement the idea?

What is my target date/deadline for implementing the idea?

How and when will I measure my success?

What's in It for Me?

"WHAT'S in it for me?" is a very logical question to ask yourself at this point. Why should I do all of these things? Where do I want to go from here?

Where you go depends totally on you. You have been exposed to a new way to view, analyze, and conduct the professional sales process. Don't just accept everything that you have read here. Instead take what makes sense to you and weave it into your current reality. Nothing that you have read in this book is cast in concrete. The chapters you choose to use and how you use them will ultimately determine your sales effectiveness—now and in the future.

We would be extremely pleased if, after reading this book, you immediately went out and started practicing the philosophy of being your own sales manager. It won't be easy though. It will take practice, some mistakes, and more practice to implement these strategies.

Can you remember when you first learned to drive a car? Before you ever learned, you were what we call an "unconscious incompetent." That is, you didn't know how to drive.

When you first went out with one of your parents, a friend, or an instructor to drive, you became a "conscious incompetent." You still couldn't drive the car, but because of your new awareness of the automobile and its parts, you were consciously aware of why you couldn't drive it. You at least were aware of what you had to learn and do to drive.

With some additional practice and guidance, you were able to become competent in driving the car. However, you had to be consciously aware of what you were doing with all the mechanical aspects of the car as well as with your body. You consciously had to turn on your blinker signals before you executed a turn. You had to remember to monitor the traffic behind you in the rearview mirror. We call this phase of learning "conscious competence."

Think of the last time you drove a car. Were you consciously aware of things we've just discussed? Of course not. Most of us, after having driven for a while, progressed to a level of "unconscious competence." This is the level where we can do something well without even thinking about it. It comes naturally.

This example holds true for your use of the sales strategies discussed in this book. You must go through the four levels of competence in order to get to the highest level—the unconscious competence level. Achieving that level means you can manage yourself and plan your sales efforts naturally and successfully. If you can get to that level, you should see a marked increase in your sales productivity. However, you must pay a price to get to the level of unconscious competence: practice, practice, practice.

This may require a change of behavior from your method of selling. If this is the case, expect to see a temporary decrease in your sales productivity initially. This is common when experiencing a behavioral change. However, after persistence and practice—and as you approach the unconscious competency level—your sales productivity will increase beyond its previous level.

Motivation

Motivation is a term you have been bombarded with for as long as you have been in sales. Sales managers are always concerned about motivating their salespeople. What exactly is motivation, and what does it mean for you, acting as your own sales manager?

Without getting into all of the theories and models of motivation, let's define it in very pragmatic terms. Motivation is a decision on your part to be your own sales manager, to expend the effort and energy to do things right, and to persist in doing them over time.

Before you make this commitment, there are three basic questions you must ask yourself:

1. If I do the things in *Be Your Own Sales Manager*, am I likely to improve my performance?
2. If I improve my performance, am I likely to be rewarded?
3. Do I value these rewards?

To be motivated, you must answer "yes" to all three questions. If you don't believe your performance will improve by doing the things advocated in this book, save your time and energy. If you feel that by buying into these principles, your performance will increase but there will be no rewards—either psychic or monetary—why do it?

Last, if you do the things and your performance increases and you are rewarded but these rewards are not consistent with your value systems—again, why do it? However, if the rewards exceed your effort and are something you value, your motivation to take action will be high. We believe this will be the case for you.

Some General Principles

Now that you are committed (at least we hope you are), there are some general principles that you must follow to maintain your level of "want to":

1. Make sure that in your mind your work is a significant and justifiable source of pride. Professional selling is a worthy career and not just a stop along the way to something bigger and better.

2. Develop some methods to provide yourself with a sense of challenge and achievement in carrying out the daily tasks associated with your job. Constantly challenge yourself to outdo yourself.

3. Develop skills and methods to recognize and reward your sense of accomplishment for "nice tries." Not all of your efforts will result in a success. Improving and learning only come from doing. Remember that success is often the result of a succession of nice tries.

4. Develop methods for career pathing your professional growth as a salesperson. You must encourage a personal sense of growth, development, and upward mobility. The treadmill syndrome will give you a sense of nothing left to learn.

5. Understand fully that *you* are the one primarily responsible for the results you produce. You must have a sense of personal commitment to achieve your results. Assume all the authority and responsibility over your job as your organization will allow. While this increases your personal risk, it also enables you to control your own destiny.

The Cultural Mind-Set of Salespeople

One of the most important ingredients that will allow you to become your own sales manager is your mind-set regarding change.

We have observed four different types of salespeople. *Apathetic* sellers refuse even to recognize that things are changing. They are doomed. *Adapting* sellers see the changes but refuse to change their way of doing things. At best, subsistence will be their standard. *Anticipating* sellers are in for above-average results given their ability to modify their business practices in consideration of their changing environment. *Activating* sellers not only take advantage of the changes but actually create them. These sellers change the way business is conducted.

Which one of these are you? The following profiles list the attitudes of salespeople in each category.

The Apathetic Seller

1. Always "too busy."
2. Accepts traditional approaches.
3. Lacks personal and professional development programs.
4. Has a high degree of job mobility—"eight positions, three years."
5. Has below-average performance regardless of criteria.
6. Focuses entirely on costs and the short run versus investing and the long run.
7. Lacks understanding of the "economic reality of a salesperson's time."

The Adapting Seller

1. Orientation is simply to "better" last year.
2. Takes line of least resistance with customers, colleagues, and management.

3. Displays casual interest in personal and professional development.
4. Implements company programs half-heartedly.
5. Pays lip-service to planning and active selling; not sure what's involved.
6. Fears making changes in practices or focus.
7. Feels that "things could be better if I could only get my act together."

The Anticipating Seller

1. Actively pursues market opportunities within the territory.
2. Believes in planning—marketing, territory, and time.
3. Has an organized approach for collecting, analyzing, and communicating information.
4. Engages in joint planning and implementation of programs with customers.
5. Participates actively in industry and community activities.
6. Committed to "stretching" personal and professional skills, as well as territory market potential.

The Activating Seller

1. Is obsessed about current and future market position.
2. Has adopted planning completely.
3. Focuses on what's most significant.
4. Discerns trends.
5. Creates changes in company and customers.
6. Is capable of "internal selling"—the ability to have the company adjust offerings to the changing marketplace.
7. Functions as a general manager of territory's market potential.

Which profile are you? Which should you be? Will you accept the challenge?

Getting Started!

As you evaluate your situation in each of the areas that we covered in this book and compare it with your new objectives, identify problem areas that need work. There may be a number of areas, but take care to set priorities on problem areas according to how much attention they need. First work on the areas that need the most help. As you become more competent, go on to the lower-priority areas. Develop an action plan specifically to improve those areas that will help you in your quest to become a strategic, professional salesperson. Define ways to accomplish your action plan. Set up an implementation schedule and follow through. Set goals and establish your criteria for success; determine how and when to measure your performance in improving your strategic selling skills. Constantly monitor your results, and take corrective action where and when necessary. Priorities, focus, intensity, goals, strategies, deadlines, and measurements are your keys to success.

Your new action plan might include professional help in the form of seminars, books, or tapes. Keep informed of ways to improve any or all of the skills discussed in this book. Your plan may also include a detailed review of relevant portions of this book.

Your skills will allow you to interact with your clients and prospects and solve their problems in an atmosphere of trust and helpfulness. Your prospects and clients will gain relevant solutions to their needs and problems. You will deservedly feel an increased pride in your new successful selling style.

You needn't wait. You can start to apply these skills immediately. Where do you go from here? Only *you* know which path you will take. Good luck!

Appendix

Assessing Your Territory's Marketplace Opportunities

IN order to understand whether you can achieve the results that your organization's and your own personal goals require, you must fully understand the opportunities in your territory. Many sellers fail to evaluate their territory's market potential. They know how much they have sold and to whom, but they do not know what that represents as a share of their market. This creates a severe problem in territory planning. These sellers do not know what they can accomplish and where their efforts should be directed. It also puts them in a disadvantaged position when they are being evaluated. How can you forecast sales or evaluate your sales quotas if you do not know what your territory can support?

Knowing your own company and products is only a part of the battle. You must also know the market of which your territory is a small part. An analysis of your territory by market segments simplifies the process. A market segment is one category or type of industry or business. For example, if you are selling copy machines, some of the market segments would be banks, libraries, hospitals, law firms, and doctor's offices. Each of these segments is different, but, within each category, the individual account's needs are quite similar.

For each market segment, you need to know the potential demand for your product in terms of gross sales and number of units to be sold. This quantitative analysis should be done for a specified period of time, usually one year. Two types of data are needed for an accurate market analysis: *market potential* and *sales potential*. Market potential is comprised of the maximum sales possible for all companies in the market. For example, how many copying machines will be sold in your territory regardless of manufacturer? Sales potential data seek to determine the maximum sales for a specific company during a given period of time.

You need to assess the sales potential in your territory for each market segment. This will help you in many ways. You will see at a glance which market segments appear to be most promising. You'll be able to rank the market segments in

THE MARKET-TARGET SEGMENT MIX				
		Market Target A	Market Target B	Market Target N	Horizontal Totals
T H E P R O D U C T M I X	Product Line 1				
	Product Line 2				
	Product Line N				
	Vertical Totals				Grand Total

order of priority and budget your time accordingly. You'll be able to set different (and therefore more realistic) objectives for each, as well as different amounts of money for promotion and personal selling efforts.

The logical approach to this analysis is to use the product/ market-target segment matrix.

The product/target market segments groupings should have been developed in your firm's marketing plan. The objective of our analysis is to evaluate the market and sales potential in each of the cells. The logic of the process is:

A Methodology for Assessing Market Potential

Some of you may be selling to industrial firms directly or through distributors, and some of you may be selling to consumers. We will provide a detailed methodology that we have used many times in the industrial market.

The industrial marketplace is defined as any firm or institution that purchases products for other than personal consumption. Selling computers or office copiers to business or motors to the after-market through distributors fall into this category. The approach that we use is based on the Standard Industrial Classification (SIC), a uniform numbering system for categorizing nearly all industries according to the type of product produced or the operation performed.

This process contains five steps:

1. Define your territory in terms of the geography in which you sell (states and counties).
2. Describe your target market segments previously identified in terms of the appropriate SIC codes.
3. Determine by targeted four-digit SIC code and county the total number of firms and employees.
4. Estimate the rate of purchase or usage by targeted four-digit SIC code of the products that you sell.

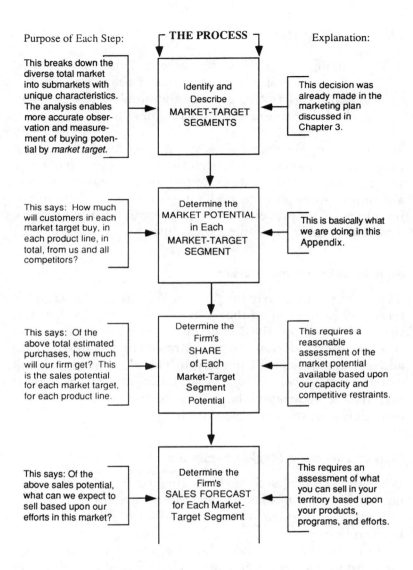

Purpose of Each Step:

THE PROCESS

Explanation:

This breaks down the diverse total market into submarkets with unique characteristics. The analysis enables more accurate observation and measurement of buying potential by *market target*.

Identify and Describe
MARKET-TARGET SEGMENTS

This decision was already made in the marketing plan discussed in Chapter 3.

This says: How much will customers in each market target buy, in each product line, in total, from us and all competitors?

Determine the
MARKET POTENTIAL
in Each
MARKET-TARGET SEGMENT

This is basically what we are doing in this Appendix.

This says: Of the above total estimated purchases, how much will our firm get? This is the sales potential for each market target, for each product line.

Determine the
Firm's
SHARE
of Each
Market-Target Segment Potential

This requires a reasonable assessment of the market potential available based upon our capacity and competitive restraints.

This says: Of the above sales potential, what can we expect to sell based upon our efforts in this market?

Determine the
Firm's
SALES FORECAST
for Each Market-Target Segment

This requires an assessment of what you can sell in your territory based upon your products, programs, and efforts.

5. Estimate the total market potential for your defined territory by multiplying the rates of usage for each targeted four-digit SIC code by the number of employees and adding this up for your total territory.

We will go into detail and show you how to develop each step in this process. Keep in mind that this procedure will not give you an estimate that is accurate to four decimal places. You are simply attempting to understand better the "size of the breadbox." This procedure will give you an information base that is invaluable to running your business.

Step 1: Defining the Market

This is the easiest step in the process. What is your geographic territory? Keep in mind that your core market is the key. You really want to assess the 20 percent of your market that gives you 80 percent of your results. Worksheet 1 is designed to address this question. Even if you have been given account assignments rather than a geographic territory, you must identify the geographic boundaries of your market. If you can't define it, you can't measure it.

Step 2: Targeting Market Segments

What are your targeted market segments? Based on the information from the marketing plan and your sales records, determine the segments that you will be selling in your marketplace.

Once you have defined these segments and described them, you must then determine which four-digit SIC codes apply to each segment.

Basically the SIC system is a uniform numbering system for classifying establishments in the United States according to the economic activity they engage in. Establishments are classified by economic activity by the Office of Management and

Worksheet 1

STEP 1: DEFINING THE GEOGRAPHIC MARKET AREA	
STATES	COUNTIES

Budget and compiled in its *Standard and Industrial Classification Manual*. This manual, which is published every five years, contains all industries classified by a four-digit SIC number and can be purchased from the U.S. Government Printing Office, Washington, D.C. 20402.

The basis of the SIC manual is relatively easy to understand. The U.S. economy is divided into eleven divisions, including one for nonclassifiable establishments. Within each division, major industry groups are classified by two-digit numbers. For example, all manufacturing firms are in division D, and two-digit numbers from 20 to 39 indicate major manufacturing industries. SIC 22 includes all manufacturers of furniture and fixtures. Thus the two-digit SIC numbers describe major or basic industries. The major industries can be further subdivided into three-, four-, five-, and seven-digit SIC numbers.

Within each major two-digit SIC industry group, industry subgroups are defined by a third digit, and detailed industries are defined by a fourth digit. This is the basis of the four-digit SIC system found in the *Standard Industrial Classification Manual*; the longer the number is, the more detailed is the industry being defined. It is also possible to supplement the four-digit SIC numbers with five- and seven-digit SIC numbers provided by the *Census of Manufacturers*.

What this means to the industrial seller is that a practical classification system for industrial customers already exists, and firms in practically every industry in the United States are already classified by appropriate SIC numbers. If you know enough about your present and potential customers to classify them into at least four-digit SIC market segments, you are halfway home in regard to locating such customers, defining their sales volumes, and determining market potential and other such considerations. Use Worksheet 2 to develop your segment descriptions by SIC codes.

Figures A-1 and A-2 provide specifics.

Figure A-1.
The Standard Industrial Classification System

Division	Two-Digit SIC Number	Major Industry Classified
A	01–09	Agriculture, forestry, fishing
B	10–14	Mining
C	15–17	Construction
D	20–39	Manufacturing
E	40–49	Transportation and other public utilities
F	50–51	Wholesale trade
G	52–52	Retail trade
H	60–67	Finance, insurance, and real estate
I	70–89	Service
J	91–97	Government

Figure A-2.
Detailed Breakdown of the SIC System

Classification	SIC Classification	Description
Division	D	Manufacturing
Major group	34	Manufacturers of fabricated metal products
Industry subgroup	344	Manufacturers of fabricated structural metal products
Specific industry	3441	Manufacturers of fabricated structural steel
Product class	34411	Manufacturers of fabricated structural metal for buildings
Product	3441121	Manufacturers of fabricated structural iron and steel for buildings

Figure A-3 provides a listing of other SIC-based data that may be of further assistance.

An additional useful tool in identifying the potential users incorporating state, county, and SIC categories is the *Sales Management Survey of Industrial Buying Power*. Figure A-4 is an example of the data available in this survey. It utilizes the SIC codes at a four-digit level, but by county and state and gives the number of plants, total shipment, the percentage of U.S. shipments, and the percentage in large plants. This tool can also be used in a similar fashion to the SIC. It may be a bit more specific in the sense that you might utilize large plants in your analysis.

Step 3: Determining Number of Employees by Target Segment and County

Using *County Business Patterns* you can now determine the number of employees by SIC code by county for your territory. Worksheet 3 is useful in this step. Look up your territory's counties and transfer the employee and firms data into this worksheet. You can buy the current *County Business Patterns* or consult a copy at a local central library in most major cities.

Step 4: Determining Rates of Usage

There are two primary sources of rate usage data: calculation of rates of usage by surveying SIC categories and calculation of rates of usage by using internal company records of past sales to various SIC categories.

Rates of Usage: Surveys

The use of a survey to determine the extent to which the various products you are examining in your market potential analysis is similar to the process of conducting a market research study. You are attempting to determine information from the respondents relative to their past purchases, in units

Worksheet 2

STEP 2: TARGETING MARKET SEGMENTS		
MARKET SEGMENT	**DESCRIPTION**	**SIC CODE(S)**
A. _____	_____ _____ _____	_____ _____ _____
B. _____	_____ _____ _____	_____ _____ _____
C. _____	_____ _____ _____	_____ _____ _____
D. _____	_____ _____ _____	_____ _____ _____

Worksheet 3

STEP 3: TARGETED FOUR-DIGIT SIC CODES				
1 STATES	2 COUNTY	3 TARGETED FOUR-DIGIT SIC CODES	4 TOTAL NO. OF EMPLOYEES	5 TOTAL NO. OF FIRMS

or dollars, of a particular type of product. In terms of their past performance or intentions for the future, the purchases are projected across all plants in a similar industry, as categorized by the SIC code, in order to calculate total market potential.

Types of Data to Obtain in the Survey
The types of data you gather in your survey regarding rates of usage might be based on the following types of questions:

1. Does your plant use, for example, air cylinders?
2. How many air cylinders were used in your plant last year?
3. What were the applications in which the air cylinders were used?
4. Please list the names of the leading or major suppliers of air cylinders to your firm.
5. Do you anticipate the use of more air cylinders in the next year?
6. If yes, how many units do you expect to buy in the next year?
7. In your plant, please list (a) total workers, (b) number of employees directly engaged in work related to the air cylinders, (c) the principal product manufactured by your plant, and (d) your primary SIC code.

Select a sample of firms in each of the SIC categories and obtain this information. You can then determine the rate of usage of the product in question as a function of the number of employees in each of the sampled plants. This will give you a rate of use factor on a per-employee basis.

Rates of Usage: Company Records
Company sales records are a good source of data for calculating market potential in terms of developing usage rates. Your past sales can be extrapolated to the entire industry consum-

FIGURE A-3.
Sources of SIC-based Data

Source	When Published	Digits of SIC Information	Type of Data
U.S. Census of Manufactures	Every five years (1982, 1987)	2-, 3-, 4-, 5-, and 7-digit data	Detailed industry information, product classes, etc.
U.S. Survey of Manufacturers	Years other than when census is	2-, 3-, 4-, and 5-digit data	Data similar to those in *Census of Manufactures* but in less detail
U.S. Industrial Outlook	Annually	2-, 3-, and 5-digit data	Number of companies where concentrated; industry trends
County Business Patterns	Annually	2-, 3-, and 4-digit data	Number of employees; taxable payrolls; totals by state and county
Sales & Marketing Management's *Survey of Industrial Purchasing Power*	Annually in Sales and Marketing Management	4-digit data	Number of plants; value of shipments; percentage of U.S. shipments by state and county

Source	Frequency	Data	Information
Private industrial directories	Annually	4-digit data	Company names and addresses; SICs; products produced; sales volumes; etc.
State/county/municipality industrial directories	Varies—some annually, some every two years	4-digit data	Company names and addresses; SICs; products produced; sales volumes; etc.
Predicasts' *Basebook* and *Forecasts*	Quarterly	7-digit data	Industry forecasts and sources by SICs
Dun & Bradstreet's *Market Identifiers*	Not published—computerized data bank	4-digit data	Company names and addresses; SICs; sales volumes; net worth; line of business, etc.
Mailing-list companies	Not published—computerized data bank	4-, 5-digit data	Mailing labels—company names and addresses; more detailed company data on request

FIGURE A-4.
Example of Data in Sales Management Survey of Industrial Purchasing Power

County SIC	Metro Area Industry	Total Plants	Large Plants	Total Shipment ($ Mil.)	% of U.S. Shipments	% In U.S. Large Plants
ALABAMA:						
Marengo	All Mfg.	15	2	169.1	.0098	68
Marion	All Mfg.	20	12	234.6	.0136	89
Marshall	116 All Mfg.	24		913.4	.0529	76
2016	Poultry-dressing plants	5	5	240.1	3.3549	100
2328	Men's & boys' work clothes	3	2	60.5	1.2757	97
2821	Plastics materials & synthetic resins	1	1	224.5	1.6370	100
Mobile	177 All Mfg.	153	50	2,684.6	.1554	76
2621	Paper mills, except building paper	2	2	565.6	3.0427	100
2819	Industrial inorganic chemicals n.e.c.	7	4	182.6	1.6956	91
3443	Fabricated plate work (boiler shops)	6	3	74.0	.8369	88
3731	Ship building & repairing	7	2	167.8	2.0517	91
Monroe	All Mfg.	14	7	236.0	.0137	82
Montgomery	180 All Mfg.	109	50	1,117.6	.0647	80

ing your products in a given geographic area. You then have a good basis for attempting to evaluate the total market potential. The necessary data inputs are the annual purchases of the product by some of your customers in the various industry categories and some estimate of your firm's share of an individual company's total purchases. You must also obtain some idea of each of your customer's total employees at the site into which you are selling this annual volume.

For example, a rate of usage calculation using company records might look like the example in Figure A-5. The statistic of $7.44 per employee for the highway and street construction group and $5.75 per employee for the heavy construction group are then used as rates of purchase. The company market share statistic was determined by asking the purchaser the extent to which we were supplying his purchases of bearings.

Worksheet 4 is a summary sheet of this process. You should be able to develop rates of purchase for each of your targeted market segments. Keep in mind that this is an estimating process but one that you can conduct with a minimum investment of time and money. *Remember, you must use Worksheet 4 for each of your product lines.* You should develop a rate of purchase for each SIC code for each of your product lines.

Step 5: Estimating Territory Market Potential

You are now at the stage of arriving at the sum total of the market potential for your territory. Worksheet 5 is a survey sheet for your territory. Once again, fill out this worksheet for each of your product lines.

Summary Table: Territory Market Potential

Using the five-step procedure just described, you now have a picture of your market opportunities. Each of the cells in the

Worksheet 4

STEP 4: RATES OF PURCHASE					
(1) Targeted Four-Digit SIC Code	(2) Firm Name	(3) Total Number of Employees	(4) Total Annual Purchases of the Types of Products We Sell	(5) 4 ÷ 3 Annual Purchases Per Employee	(6)* Average Annual Purchases Per Employee by 4-Digit SIC Code

* To calculate (6) annual purchases per employee by four-digit SIC code, you add the total annual purchases and the total number of employees for each four-digit SIC code. Divide the sum total of the annual purchases by the sum total number of employees.

250

Figure A-5.
Product: Bearings

	SIC	Firm	Total Annual Sales	Company Market Share	Total Purchases	Total Employment in Customer Plant	Per Employee
Motor vehicle manufacturers	3711	Ajax	50,000	.60	$ 83,333	11,000	$7.58
		Boron	10,000	.80	125,000	17,000	7.35
TOTAL					$208,333	28,000	$7.44
Machine tool, metal-forming types, mfrs.	3542	Cut-Rite	22,000	.40	$ 55,000	9,500	$5.78
		Delta	8,000	.20	40,000	7,000	5.71
TOTAL					$ 95,000	16,500	$5.75

251

Worksheet 5

STEP 5: SALES POTENTIAL BY COUNTY AND TARGETED SIC CODE

1	2	3	4	5	6 (4 x 5)
State	County	Targeted 4-Digit SIC Code	Total No. of Employees by SIC Code	Average Annual Purchases Per Employee by Sic Code	Sales Potential for SIC Codes by County

NOTES: To estimate potential sales for any given SIC code you will have to sort the results (column 6) from this worksheet.

To estimate potential sales by county, simply add the potential for each targeted SIC code in the county.

matrix should now have a market potential number. The following hypothetical example illustrates the point.

Using the steps in the procedure, we have calculated the market potential for Mary's territory in Northwest Ohio to be:

Mary now has a good idea of where her major opportunities are in terms of market potential. These market potentials form the basis for most territory planning.

Where Do You Go from Here?

What do you do with your market potentials? First, determine whether your territory is capable of generating the numbers that your personal goals and your organization re-

		THE MARKET-TARGET SEGMENT MIX			
		Medical	Financial	Educational	Product Line Totals
T H E	Computers	1,500,000	6,000,000	2,500,000	10,000,000
P R O D U C T	Software	900,000	4,000,000	1,500,000	6,000,000
	Office Machines	600,000	2,000,000	1,000,000	4,000,000
M I X	Segment Totals	3,000,000	12,000,000	5,000,000	20,000,000

* Data are in dollars

quire. A second major value of these potentials is that they give you a base for planning your selling efforts.

Let's evaluate your organizational goals in the light of these market potentials.

Using Mary's territory potentials, sales objectives in total for each product line, actual sales, and sales objectives for each target segment by each product line, Mary can make some judgments as to whether her 1990 sales objectives are reasonable.

Based on these actual sales dollars, future sales objectives, and market potentials, Mary can make some judgments regarding whether the 1990 sales objectives are realistic.

Let's initially examine software in the financial market segment. Keep in mind that we are looking at the face value of the numbers. Mary should have had some inputs to the original setting of the 1990 sales objectives since there are many qualifying elements, such as the economic and competitive

	1990 SALES OBJECTIVE		1989 ACTUAL SALES	
	$ (000)	%	$ (000)	%
COMPUTERS	1,750	50%	1,800	60%
SOFTWARE	1,050	30%	600	20%
OFFICE MACHINES	700	20%	1600	20%
TOTAL	3,500	**100%**	3,000	**100%**

• **Place your total sales objective here**

• **Current year actual sales**

TARGET MARKET
SEGMENTS (000)

PRODUCT LINE	MEDICAL		FINANCIAL		EDUCATIONAL		TOTAL	
	1990	1989	1990	1989	1990	1989	1990	1989
COMPUTERS $	391	400	875	900	484	600	1,750	1,800
SOFTWARE $	350	150	450	250	250	200	1,050	600
OFFICE MACHINES $	125	100	450	400	125	100	700	600
$	866	650	1,775	1,550	859	900	$3,500	$3,000

1990 TOTAL SALES OBJECTIVE ⬆

1989 ACTUAL SALES ⬆

FINANCIAL SEGMENT
SOFTWARE

	Estimated Market Potential	Sales	Market Share
1989	4,000,000	250,000	6.25%
1990	4,000,000	450,000	11.25%

New Market Share Required	=	6.25%
Current Market Share	=	11.25%
Additional Percentage Points	=	5.00

But $\dfrac{5.00 \text{ the gain}}{6.25 \text{ the present}}$ = 80%

255

climate in his territory. All we want to pass judgment on at this time is whether Mary feels that the numbers are realistic.

The question that Mary has to address is whether an 80 percent increase in market share is feasible. In reality, the market potential for 1990 would probably have increased and the increase in market share would not be so drastic. However, the logic is correct. Mary must now look at her accounts (existing and potential) in the financial segment to see where the additional software sales might be forthcoming.

Each cell should undergo the same scrutiny. The market share increases for the entire territory look like the following:

Chapter 4 provides the tools to evaluate these market share changes. You and Mary will have to develop a marketing plan for your territory and based upon that information develop your sales program.

You have now addressed the priorities for you personally and for your firm. The analysis that you should have conducted is the third pillar in our triangle (see Figure 2-2). Do you feel that your personal and organizational objectives can be accomplished given the market potentials in your territory?

TARGET MARKET SEGMENTS

PRODUCT LINE	MEDICAL	FINANCIAL	EDUCATIONAL	TOTAL
COMPUTERS	2.3% ↓	2.8% ↓	19.3% ↓	2.8% ↓
SOFTWARE	134% ↑	80% ↑	25% ↑	75% ↑
OFFICE MACHINES	25% ↑	12.5% ↑	25% ↑	16.7% ↑
TOTAL	38.5% ↑	19.4% ↑	11.1% ↑	16.7% ↑

You can identify strategic gaps in your selling efforts based on the existence or nonexistence of market potential. You can deploy your sales efforts better by understanding the physical portion of your territory's potentials—an extremely critical step in becoming a better manager of sales.

INDEX